"That Was a Pin?"

"That Was a Pin?"

The Story of SPRINT CORP.
An inside view of the 100-year history of a once-great company — from its humble beginnings to a rather ignominous end

**By
John R. Hoffman**

Copyright © 2000 John R. Hoffman

Copyright 2000
Printed in the United States

ISBN: 1-58597-028-X

Library of Congress Catalog Card No.00-090538

Leathers Publishing
4500 College Blvd.
Leawood, KS 66211
Phone: 1/888/888-7696

TABLE OF CONTENTS

Page

Preface

Chapter One: In the Beginning 1

Chapter Two: The Company Reinvents Itself 13

Chapter Three: US Sprint 25

Chapter Four: Sprint Corp. 39

Chapter Five: The Telecom Act 55

Chapter Six: Wireless, International and ION 81

Chapter Seven: Pending Industry Issues 97

Chapter Eight: The Merger 113

Chapter Nine: Conclusion 129

Photographs 138

About the Author 169

Index 171

PREFACE

I have long believed that the story of Sprint Corp. should and someday would be told in America's business schools, because it's a remarkable success story. From my perspective, it's a story of what was done right (and not-so-right) to build a successful competitor from a rather small and comfortable monopoly. It seems like a good time to tell the story, now that I've retired from active employment with Sprint, and now that the story is about to end.

I need to emphasize that this version of the story is a very personal memoir (and not officially authorized by Sprint). While I have diligently tried to stick to the facts set forth herein, I readily admit that they are influenced by my personal involvement and perspective. I learned early in my career that that there are few unequivocal facts; most facts are affected by the view of the beholder. In that regard, most of the facts and observations herein are from my own recollections, calendars and files, although I used published articles, annual reports, Sprint's Web site and other public sources to try to confirm my recollections.

I also have to especially admit my personal bias with respect to a number of people. At the heart of the Sprint story are a variety of people. Some are, in their own way, remarkable and responsible for Sprint's success, and I hope I've treated them fairly and with due respect. Some I don't hold in high regard, but I've tried not to use this book to criticize or "get even" with (or even identify) them. I simply want to make the point that (contrary to what I used to believe) the success of even a large corporation can be affected by individuals. Good ones can have an enormously positive impact, while bad ones unfortunately can and often do cause disproportionate harm.

In any event, I have to begin by thanking my family. I started work as a summer clerk in 1967 (after I graduated from college, but before I started law school) at the company that became Sprint because of the relationship between my parents and Paul Henson. My parents gave me a lot, including good direction toward a rewarding career. The year I started work full-time, 1970, was also when I got married. My wife, Linda, tolerated my workaholic ways for almost 30 years. If I achieved any success in that time, I owe it all to her and my daughter, Heather (born in 1973). One of the main reasons I retired (in 1999) was to give them the time and attention they deserve for the next 30 years.

CHAPTER ONE

In the Beginning

THE STORY OF SPRINT began 100 years ago. It started slowly. For the first half of its existence, the corporate entity that would become today's Sprint Corp. was a privately-owned quaint, independent utility serving small, rural towns in the Midwest.

But the next three generations of leadership — Skip Scupin, Paul Henson and Bill Esrey (each of which, interestingly, personally recruited his successor from outside the company) — brought professional management, technological savvy, a penchant for growth, extraordinary people skills and a vision for the future of the industry and the company. They transformed the company from a sleepy little monopoly into a competitive powerhouse. Sprint, as a result, is today one of the best known and respected brands in the telecommunications industry.

The transformation was not easy; indeed, it was hard on employees, stockholders and, for awhile, customers. But it was worth it. Sprint is now bigger, stronger, focused, determined and, perhaps, one of the best positioned companies in the industry to win in the global market.

Sprint is, also, being taken over by one of its arch-rivals, MCI/WorldCom. If consummated, the merger — amounting to $129 billion, including debt — will be one of the largest in the history of corporate America (exceeded, so far, only by the $141-billion AOL-Time Warner combination, announced in January 2000). There is some reason to expect that the merger will not be completed in its original form, due to conditions likely to be imposed by regulators or even the possibility of hostile offers for Sprint; but if it does, the life of Sprint (as we have come, especially in recent years, to know it) will come to a rather ignominious end. The good news is that

Sprint stockholders (particularly long-time investors) will be amply rewarded for their faith and persistence. In any event, now seems like a good time to tell the story of Sprint. Let me begin at the beginning.

Brown Telephone Company

Cleyson L. Brown was an entrepreneur in Abilene, Kansas, who sought to serve a number of community needs. He and his brother, Jacob, started a water company to serve the town, then used a water wheel to generate electricity. In October 1899, the Browns decided to use their wires and poles to provide telephone service (priced at $1.00 per month, compared to Bell's $3.00 residential rate).

Alexander Graham Bell, as every child learns in school, invented the telephone in 1876. He patented the invention, formed the American Telephone Company, and began to wire every major city in the United States for local service (and eventually connected them via "Long Lines" to provide long distance service). The patent and renewal rights gave Bell a monopoly over telephone service for over 25 years; but after the turn of the century smaller non-Bell companies (known as "Independent" telephone companies) were formed by individual entrepreneurs to provide service in communities in rural and suburban areas that had been ignored by Bell.

The Brown Telephone Company, in particular, was chartered in 1902. By 1911 it served 4,111 telephones in and around Abilene. That year it consolidated with other Independent telephone companies in Kansas to form the United Telephone Company. Over time, Brown acquired all or parts of 68 water, electric and (mostly) telephone companies, and in 1925 formed a holding company, United Telephone & Electric (UT&E). The company largely survived the Great Depression in 1929, but lost many telephone customers (and, thus, revenues) to the poor economy in subsequent years. Brown's health also declined, and in 1934 the company filed for reorganization under the bankruptcy laws. By 1937, the company had recovered and continued to expand. In 1939, the holding company's name was changed to United Utilities, Incorporated ("UUI").

United Utilities, Incorporated

Carl A. "Skip" Scupin had been hired by Brown in 1921, and led the effort to modernize and expand UUI. In 1959, Skip became President and commenced to move the company's headquarters to Kansas City. One of the reasons for the move was to attract better talent to the company, and one of Skip's premier acquisitions was a young man from Lincoln, Nebraska, named Paul H. Henson. Paul worked his way through the University of Nebraska (his college education was interrupted from 1943-45, when he served as a pilot in the U.S. Air Force) by climbing poles at Lincoln Telephone & Telegraph Company. He served as a Warehouseman, District Engineer and Chief Engineer at LT&T, and came to UUI as Vice President-Operations.

United Telephone System

Paul worked tirelessly in the early 1960s to convert the United Telephone Companies owned by UUI (known as the United Telephone System, or UTS) to dial operation. (As an interesting aside, the dial telephone was invented by a Kansas City funeral director named Almon B. Strowger to prevent an operator — who was the girlfriend of his competitor — from referring operator-handled calls to his competitor) and to establish sales operations. The company's first headquarters in Kansas City were located in the VFW Building on Broadway.

Paul's work ethic was legendary and, as a consequence, his young daughters (Susan and Beth), due in part to their Swedish heritage, thought those initials stood for "Vere Father Worked." Paul's efforts paid off; revenue and earnings increased by more than 10% a year, and in 1961 UUI was named one of the best values in communications stocks by *Financial World* magazine.

Paul also moved the company's offices to the suburbs. He bought a Hallmark Cards warehouse at the corner of Johnson Drive (now Shawnee Mission Parkway) and Rainbow (actually, a gas station occupied the corner, and the warehouse parking lot wrapped around it) in Westwood, Kansas, and converted it into a two-story office building. The entire company moved in — the parent company (UUI) occupying the second floor, and the United Telephone System-Midwest Group (headed by J.G. "Skinny" Kreamer, a legend in the telephone industry) on the first floor — in the mid-1960s. As the company grew, it quietly but persistently acquired the other properties on the block (including the gas station, which is now a beautiful garden), and in the late 1970s started constructing a headquarters building that stretches from Rainbow to Belinder. (It is, in effect, a high-rise office building — that would have been a vertical eyesore in the neighborhood — lying on its side). The new building (which preserved parts of the old warehouse in the southeast corner) was finished and occupied in the early 1980s, and remains a cornerstone of both the company (the executive offices — which were originally and beautifully decorated by Betty Henson — are still there) and the community. It is one of the two buildings (the other is at Nall and College Blvd.) that the company owns, but will likely be sold when the new Campus in Overland Park, Kansas is finished.

In 1964, Skip retired and was succeeded by Paul as President of UUI. Paul reorganized the company to achieve efficiencies through centralization, and embarked upon an ambitious acquisition campaign called "Growth Through Additions" with the goals of amassing 2 million telephone lines and $1 billion in assets. He, personally, flew around the country negotiating deals and by 1966 had doubled the size of the United Telephone System by acquiring companies in Ohio, Oregon, Tennessee, Virginia and Pennsylvania. By 1969, Paul had doubled the size of the company again, with more acquisitions in Florida, Texas and North and South Carolina.

Continental Telephone

Other independent telephone companies were also consolidating at the time and, in particular, Paul was in competition with Continental Telephone Company. Continental was, itself, an interesting story because it was created to take advantage of the merger activity in the industry at the time. Phil Lucier worked with my father at Stromberg Carlson Corp. selling equipment to Independent telephone companies (since AT&T's subsidiary, Western Electric, was at the time prohibited by an antitrust decree — known as the Kingsbury Commitment — from selling to non-Bell companies). He was an energetic and ambitious young man, and a good family friend. He loved Lincoln Continental automobiles and bought a new one every year. I vividly remember as a youngster when Phil would visit my Dad, that he'd let us crawl all over and admire his new car.

Phil persuaded Charles Wholstetter, a New York financier, to back his plan to acquire and consolidate small Independent telephone companies across the nation to gain size, stature and economies of scale. He named the holding company Continental Telephone Co. (after, I always believed, his beloved automobiles) and soon became the third largest Independent telephone company (behind GTE and United Telephone) in the country. Phil was tragically (and ironically) killed in 1970 by a car bomb (that, it was later learned, was intended for someone else) and several years later

Wholstetter sold the company to GTE.

While Phil was building Continental, he and Paul Henson often crossed paths as they competed for the affection and affiliation of several Independent telephone properties. They were friends, but the atmosphere was not particularly friendly when they met in small town airports as one was coming and the other was leaving from meetings with shareholders of attractive and available companies.

There's little doubt that the premiums paid for some of those companies (which made some rural families very wealthy) were due in large measure to the desire of Paul and Phil to beat one another. It was cause for celebration at UUI when it outbid Continental to acquire another Independent telephone company.

The United Family

By 1970, Paul had achieved his growth objectives and began to mold this diverse company into a cohesive and focused operating unit. His approach, in addition to setting high standards (and always leading by example), was to move people from the newly acquired telephone companies into headquarters and to replace them in the field with headquarters staff. This process not only developed better and more rounded employees, but built a genuine United "family." Indeed, Paul ran the company much like a family. He made it a point to not only know each of the employees, but their spouses and children as well. And it wasn't a gimmick; he genuinely cared for people and wanted them to enjoy good lives both at and away from the office.

I remember with great fondness the annual address Paul would make to the employees' Christmas luncheon. Back in those days, the company was small enough that all headquarters employees could gather on Christmas Eve in a Kansas City hotel meeting room for lunch, listen to Paul's annual homily, receive a gift and go home early to be with our families. Paul's remarks were always the highlight, and they stayed with all of us for a long time. He always spoke from the heart about the condition of the company, the country, the world, and mankind. He always educated and touched everyone, and we would have done anything for that man.

How I Got Started

My father (Raymond E. Hoffman) succeeded my grandfather (Raymond O. Hoffman) in the headquarters of Stromberg Carlson in Rochester, New York. I was born in Rochester in 1945 (the second of four boys) and we moved to Chicago three years later when my dad became head of that district office. We returned to Rochester ten years later, and moved again to Kansas City in 1961 when my dad was named to head that district office. His biggest customer was the United Telephone System, and I got to know the Henson family. That relationship gave direction to the rest of my life.

My family heritage probably accounts for (as well as my middle name) my extended career at Sprint. My father and grandfather worked their entire careers for one company, and it was always a source of pride to me to give my employer unquestioned loyalty and commitment. And both Sprint and my assignments changed often enough to always make the work challenging and satisfying. But the employment world changed around me, and I became a dinosaur.

These days almost no one works for the same company for their entire career. Instead, dramatic career advancements are most often achieved by changing employers. I don't find fault in that development; I recognize that it's driven by changes in the global economy, technology and the demographics of the workforce. Yet I feel some regret for the young people today who will never experience or benefit from the perspective that can be gained from a lifetime of relationships with leaders like Paul Henson.

When Paul retired in 1990, the company published a number of moving tributes to him and his family. I thought a long time about how to express my appreciation and admiration for him, and wrote a letter to try to explain the impact he'd had upon me. In that letter, I told him a story that I'd never before shared with anyone. I was in college when Paul became President of UUI and, because I'd met (through my parents) his family, I read with great interest an article about him in the "Sunday Features" of the December 5, 1965 issue of the *Kansas City Star*. Paul was quoted as saying, among other things, that:

> *"There's simply not enough of the Christian ethic in business today ... You can conduct business affairs in a genteel Christian manner — and regard people as individual human beings rather than numbers ... It's a matter of applying the Golden Rule ... In this company, we welcome anyone in here with an idea or a suggestion ..."*

I was 20 years old at the time and still somewhat impressionable, and Paul's philosophy deeply affected me. It was the first time

I'd heard of a successful business executive advocating treating people in the office just the same as though he would in church. He believed that all people should at all times be treated with fairness, dignity, respect and compassion, unless and until they did something to deserve less.

Paul's words moved me. I wanted to work for that man. In 1967, when I graduated from college, he gave me a job as a summer intern. I mostly fetched pencils, moved desks and other odd jobs, but I loved every minute of it. The people were friendly, bright and hardworking. They became my second family. I was eager to return the next summer, after my first year of law school, but I was to have a new boss.

In 1968, Paul hired Warren Baker to become the company's first in-house General Counsel. Warren had been General Counsel of the United States Independent Telephone Association (USITA) and General Counsel of the FCC. As the Washington partner of a prestigious New York law firm, Warren had tried the momentous antitrust lawsuit of the AFL vs. NFL, which resulted in the consolidation of the NFL and the creation of the Super Bowl. His relationship with Lamar Hunt was probably responsible for my undying fan support for the Kansas City Chiefs (the former Dallas Texans, who Hunt moved to K.C. in the early 1960s). Warren was a fascinating and imposing man, and taught me more about antitrust and communications law than I ever learned in law school.

In 1970, I got married, went to work full-time for UUI and finished law school at night. It was an exciting time; I worked on acquisitions, equity and bond financings, pole attachment agreements and related regulatory proceedings, and a couple of antitrust cases (where we competed against CATV operators in United Telephone operating territories). Warren taught me to pay attention to the facts and try to absorb as much about the business as possible. He believed that a corporate lawyer's contribution should include business judgment, as well as legal advice. He was a thoughtful mentor, who gave me tools that would serve me well for the rest of my career.

UTS-Southeast Group

In the early 1970s, while Paul was moving operating people to and from the field, Warren decided to place lawyers in each of the operating units. In 1975, I was sent to the United Telephone System-Southeast Group in Bristol, Tennessee. I served as the first in-house

General Counsel of those operations, providing telephone service in parts of Tennessee, Virginia, North and South Carolina, for five years. When I went, I was a know-it-all young lawyer. I quickly learned that I knew almost nothing about the technology or commitment that it took to provide telephone service.

Moreover, I was there at a difficult time. Besides the fact that there was double-digit inflation (which caused the company to have to file for rate increases in all four states almost twice a year), the company's service had been horrible. The year before I arrived, the company had installed the first digital switch in the United Telephone System, and it failed miserably. The community of Bristol, Virginia was completely without telephone service for days and weeks at a time. That gave the company a lasting bad reputation. In fact, the company (the full legal name was United Inter-Mountain Telephone Company) was often referred to in the community as the "United Intermittent Telephone Company." In self-defense, the folks that worked for the company tended to surround and protect one another, and there was a genuine sense of family.

I learned a great deal in the five years I spent in Tennessee about the telephone business, about the practice of law (I tried everything from rate cases to rape cases — there were, truly, a couple instances where lonely housewives accused our servicemen of installing more than telephones), and about human nature. It was at times intense, but it may have been the most rewarding time of my career.

Ed Smail was president of the company when I went to Tennessee. He was a brilliant and fascinating man. His father was an investor who started one of the first public utility holding companies (Ed used to tell stories about watching his father testify before Congress when the Public Utility Holding Company Act was being considered). Ed owned and operated a small telephone company in North Carolina that was acquired by UUI. He took an executive position in Kansas City (where I first met him) for a while, then headed the Southeast Group when it was formed.

Ed taught me a great deal about both the telephone business (he encouraged me to ride along with repairmen on occasion) and management of people. I also learned a lot about family and estate law as a result of working for Ed — he lost his beloved first wife to cancer shortly after we moved to Tennessee. He subsequently remarried (requiring a pre-nuptial agreement), and died of a sudden heart attack (and I worked with his family lawyers on his considerable estate).

The passing of Ed and his first wife were not the only times I had to deal with death in Tennessee. John Wilson, Vice President—Administration of the company, was a proud and elegant man who had served with great distinction as a tank commander in World War II. For reasons I never fully understood, though, he suffered from bouts of depression. He was hospitalized for a couple months; and, on the day he returned to the office (his office adjoined mine), he met with some old friends and shot himself. It was a tragic day that I'll never forget. Most of my memories, though, are of his widow, Mary Ellen, with whom I subsequently spent a lot of time settling John's estate. She was a strong and wonderful woman, who taught me a great deal about faith and surviving tragedy.

Ed Smail was replaced by W.W. ("Dub") Hill. Dub had been a Commissioner on the Indiana PSC, had run for the Republican nomination for Governor of that state, and was hired by Warren Baker as a regulatory lawyer in Kansas City (where I first met him). He came to Tennessee during an active time for rate cases, and he taught me a lot about dealing with regulators. I recall a specific instance when his tempered approach helped me through a difficult situation.

A candidate for election to the Tennessee PSC — Bobby Clement — campaigned on the promise that he would never vote for a rate increase for United Inter-Mountain Telephone Company. When he won, I prepared a petition to recuse him from all our future cases, because the statute required that he not make a decision on any matter before hearing all the evidence. I took the draft petition to Nashville and shared a copy with the PSC's General Counsel. I told him I didn't want to file it, but was genuinely concerned about Commissioner Clement's apparent prejudice against our company. The General Counsel talked to the Commissioner, and informed me that he was considering having me disbarred for trying to improperly influence his vote. I was panicked and wanted to fight back, but Dub counseled me to exercise restraint. After some time passed, Clement and I met and reconciled, and for years thereafter were friends. Bobby now represents the 5th District of Tennessee in the U.S. Congress.

Lawyering was not always so intense in those days, though. I had some great experiences and good times. I remember one instance, in particular, that was genuinely fun. We were prosecuting one of many rate cases in South Carolina, and one of my tasks was to cross-examine the Public Service Commission's (PSC's) expert economics witness. In those days, the heart of a rate case was the contest between the PSC's and the company's expert witnesses over how much profit the company should be allowed to earn (in the absence of competition). The questions usually challenged each expert's subjective judgment and the process was relatively academic (the PSC usually chose a number somewhere in between the two) and mostly routine.

But, in this case, the PSC's expert had listed among his considerable credentials the fact that he had previously testified in another case involving the company in another state, when I knew (since I had prosecuted that case, also) that he had actually withdrawn at the last minute and sent a young associate to testify in his place. I challenged the veracity of his entire testimony on the basis of this one falsehood and moved that it be stricken. The attack was unprecedented and caused quite an uproar in the hearing room. The PSC denied my motion (while pledging to give weight to my attack on his credibility in their final decision) and allowed the expert to continue testifying, but he was clearly shaken. I suspect he was much more careful about the details in his future testimony, and I certainly learned about the benefits of careful preparation.

I also got my first taste of unions in the UTS-Southeast Group. Craft people have historically been unionized in the telecommunications industry, and Northeast Tennessee (known locally as "Upper East Tennessee") was a union hotbed. I remember seeing the poverty in some small towns caused by factories that had been closed by strikes, and being puzzled by the pride of the unemployed workers for what they'd accomplished. We had a 30-day strike at the telephone company the last year I was there. The union chose to strike rather than accept a new contract offer, although I thought the terms were fair.

The union had not struck the company for decades before, and I became convinced that they were more interested in taking advantage of their sizeable strike fund (thereby getting an unscheduled but paid vacation) than achieving any justice. Regardless, emotions ran high and there was sporadic vandalism, which caused me to spend a lot of time in different courts seeking injunctions and other remedies. When it was over, some of the union leaders came to me to mend fences. The best I could do was promise to forgive, but not forget. I'd always believed that unions served a worthwhile purpose in the workplace, but my impression these days is that some unions operate for the benefit of the leadership, not the membership.

There were also a lot of good times in Tennessee. People like Dick Cashwell (who was VP-Operations, and later an Executive-VP in Florida, and President of UTS-Midwest Group), Charles Browning (who was Dick's assistant and, later, his successor), Louis Corning (as VP-Revenues, we worked together on many rate cases), Luther Wolf (VP-Finance) and many more were a joy to work with. Even though we were outsiders, they took us in and made us feel a part of their family.

At times, though, it got a little silly. Bristol was a five-hour drive from each of the state capitols — Nashville, TN; Richmond, VA; Columbia, SC, and Raleigh, NC. Spending that much time in the car on the way to meet with state officials, we got to know each other pretty well. On one of my first trips to Richmond, VA, Dick Cashwell and Luther Wolfe decided, unbeknownst to me, to initiate me into the club. At the end of the two-day trip, we got home late in the evening. I tossed my suitcase on the bed, opened it and was struck by the overwhelming smell of cheap perfume. They had placed in my suitcase (apparently while it was in the trunk of the car) an oversized, well-worn, old, smelly, pink woman's nightgown.

Thankfully, my wife trusted me (or at least believed that if I was going to be unfaithful, it would not be with such a large woman) and immediately recognized it was a joke. After some deliberation, we decided the best way to retaliate was to pretend that it never happened. We didn't say a word to Dick or Luther (and hoped that it drove them nuts). Instead, we preserved the nightgown (in all its smelly glory), gift-wrapped it and presented it to Dick at his going-away party three years later. We all got a long and long-delayed laugh. Humor enabled us to both keep our sanity and build life-long friendships. We still stay in touch with Dick, Luther and other good friends and their families from Bristol.

After five wonderful years in Tennessee, in 1980 I was promoted to VP-General Counsel of the United Telephone System and returned to Kansas City. The move was part of a rather significant reorganization that was the precursor of today's Sprint.

CHAPTER TWO

The Company Reinvents Itself

THE POPULAR consultant-speak today, when a company changes strategic course, is that it's "reinventing" itself. The company that became Sprint did that, in different degrees, several times; not because it was trendy, but because it was necessary to survive and thrive in a changing environment.

United Telecom

Paul Henson understood that the industry was facing change, and the company began to try to position itself for that change. In 1972 (after the company had sold off all remaining water and electric properties), the name of the holding company was changed from UUI to United Telecommunications, Inc. (United Telecom) to better reflect the primary business mission. It then began to pursue a number of telecommunications-related opportunities.

To the outsider, the company's experiments in different areas must have looked like uncoordinated fits-and-starts, but there was some method to the madness. Paul's inclination was to learn by doing, rather than studying alternatives. For instance, they started a company to remotely monitor alarm services (Uniwatch) and another to provide on-site alarm services (United Telesentinel), both of which were subsequently sold.

They also tried their hand at retail storefront sales of personal computers (through a subsidiary named AmeriSource), but it never made money and was short-lived. A venture to sell telephone equipment (telephones, key systems, small PBXs, etc.) to small and medium-sized businesses (called Utelcom) lasted a little longer, and taught the company about the pitfalls of aggressive competition in narrow-margin markets.

Uninet was the company's modestly successful foray into the high-speed data business, and provided insight to the long distance market. That subsidiary was consolidated with GTE's Telenet when US Sprint was formed in 1986, and remains a cornerstone of Sprint's operational excellence today.

United TeleSpectrum

United Telecom also formed a subsidiary to take advantage of the new mobile telephone services market, created when in 1980 the FCC (after almost a decade of trials and regulatory delay) finally awarded cellular licenses to incumbent local telephone companies and non-wireline competitors. Many Independent telephone companies (including United Telephone) served suburban areas (that once, prior to urban sprawl, had been rural areas) that were integral to urban cellular markets, so the Bell Companies were interested in partnering or trading cellular licenses in order to be able to provide comprehensive and seamless service.

The Independent telephone companies joined together to negotiate a standard agreement with AT&T for cellular partnerships. We usually met in Centel's offices in Chicago, and I was often offended by the fact that whereas the Independents were usually represented by a single lawyer, AT&T always showed up with a half dozen or more lawyers. It did not suggest that AT&T was preparing to be a low-cost competitor.

In any event, United Telephone (led by Bob Snedaker) carefully and craftily traded and negotiated license rights to position its new subsidiary (United TeleSpectrum) as a major industry player (by serving not only United Telephone territories but trading for minority rights in larger markets, such as Kansas City, Orlando and New York City). The commitment to cellular was genuine, but the subsidiary was subsequently sold under unusual circumstances. Central Telephone Company (Centel), headquartered in Chicago, was fending off a hostile takeover attempt and offered to buy United TeleSpectrum at a massive premium (with the expectation that the debt would be an effective "poison pill").

The price (about $750 million) was a multiple of United Telecom's investment and constituted an offer that literally couldn't be refused, especially during a time when United Telecom needed cash to fund the launch of the long distance fiber optic network. So United Telecom sold the cellular operations, but never took its eye off the wireless market. In fact, when United Telecom merged with

Centel in 1995, it re-acquired those cellular properties (plus those owned separately by Centel).

At the time, however, the next generation of cellular — known as Personal Communications Systems (PCS) — was being developed, and the FCC decided (since the award of dual cellular licenses had not produced the desired level of competition) to auction multiple PCS licenses in each market. Part of the initial FCC rules prohibited holders of cellular licenses from bidding for the new PCS licenses (to prevent incumbents from buying, warehousing and thereby precluding competing licenses). United Telecom believed in the future of PCS, so it decided to spin off the cellular properties in order to be eligible to acquire PCS licenses anywhere and everywhere. Just prior to the spin-off of United TeleSpectrum (which was re-named 360 Degrees Communications and later acquired by AllTel), the FCC's rule was struck down by the Courts; but United Telecom proceeded with its strategy anyway. More about that later.

United Computing Systems

Another, and perhaps the most telling example, was the company's foray into remote computing. To take advantage of the advances in mainframe computer technology, and the fact that telephone lines were the principal means to access this new computing power, the company acquired a nascent remote computing company in Kansas City and formed a new commercial subsidiary (United Computing Systems, or UCS). It upgraded the facilities to one of the largest computers available (Cray), and leased "dumb" terminals to customers who paid for time to process data on the large mainframe (which they, individually, couldn't afford to own). Customers ranged from small enterprises, who processed payrolls and other accounting functions, to large automakers, who performed CAD-CAM functions (requiring massive amounts of computer power).

It was a great business plan, but it completely missed the impending sharp left turn that the computer industry took into personal computers (PCs). The ability and capacity of PCs to perform desktop computing at the whim of the user (rather than having to purchase fixed blocks of time on a remote computer) dramatically and quickly changed the whole nature of the market. UCS virtually failed almost overnight (and its assets were subsequently sold to Control Data Corp.). It was an expensive but important lesson. Paul swore that the company would never again be surprised by market shifts, and made a number of changes to be better prepared for the future. He recruited and hired the company's first Chief Technology Officer, and began developing relationships with industry analysts and consultants.

Strategic Reorganization

In particular, he retained McKinsey & Co to conduct an overall evaluation of the company's strengths and weaknesses and, based thereon, to recommend a future course. It was a prolonged and very revealing process, and produced a number of strategic and organizational changes. United Telecom became a pure holding company, and three new divisions were eventually formed: (1) the United Telephone System, containing all of the local operating telephone properties, (2) a diversified group, with the equipment wholesale, directories and other businesses, and (3) a new group to pursue competitive opportunities.

Paul also hired Bill Esrey as the company's VP-Finance (and later Strategic Planning) to direct these changes. Bill's father, Todd, had headed AT&T's operation in Kansas City for years (indeed, he was known in K.C. as "Mr. Telephone"). Bill, after receiving a Harvard MBA in 1964, went to work for AT&T, eventually becoming the youngest head of an AT&T subsidiary that operated underground conduit in New York City. Seeking more challenges, Bill left AT&T and worked for Dillon Read & Co. (New York City investment bankers), becoming a protégé to Nicholas Brady (who became Treasury Secretary under President Reagan). Paul persuaded Bill to return to Kansas City and gave him the opportunity to prove that he should eventually run the company.

Bill is in many ways very different than was Paul. Paul was an extraordinary "people person," who cared very deeply about the personal impact of his business decisions. Bill is very much a "numbers guy," who approaches business in a very impersonal, calculated manner. Bill believes people are important, but they are replaceable. Bill has a very definite vision for the future of the company and is not easily, if at all, deterred in his determination to pursue the realization of that vision.

Many employees who knew and loved Paul miss him and regret that Bill lacks his compassion; but they have overlooked the fact that Paul knew Bill had the business disposition necessary to take the company to the next level of success. There's no question that the company — its employees, customers and, especially, stockholders — is better off today because of Bill's leadership (and Bill is among the first to give due credit and respect to Paul for his foresight). Bill succeeded Paul as President in 1984, and as Chairman in 1990.

US Telecom

Bill's career has been marked by bold moves, and his first was courageous. He basically rejected McKinsey's bottom-line recommendation to aggressively enter the Cable TV market and, instead, decided the company should compete against AT&T in the long distance market. The company had acquired an Atlanta-based satellite reseller (ISACOMM, which had provided long distance data services to an insurance services provider, ISA). Bill took their sales and technology expertise and started to build a long distance competitor (initially called United Telecom Communications, Inc., or UTCI). He spearheaded the acquisition of US Telephone (a Dallas-based reseller), and combined the operations into a subsidiary called US Telecom.

On August 29, 1984, I was very comfortable in the job of VP-General Counsel of UTS, working for Art Krause, when Bill Esrey asked me to lunch. Over sandwiches at the Mission Hills Country Club, he told me about his plans for succeeding in the competitive long distance market and asked me to join his team as Senior VP-General Counsel of UTCI. I was impressed with Bill, but I'd spent almost 15 years in the local telephone business and was still skeptical of competition. I did not give him an answer, but when we returned to the office Paul called me. Bill, knowing how to get what he wanted and knowing that I deeply respected and always followed Paul's advice, had gone to Paul to lobby me to take the job offer. I did, and the amount and intensity of my work dramatically and almost instantly changed.

US Telephone

US Telephone was a real eye-opener for me. The company had been started by a handful of former Braniff Airlines executives (after its first bankruptcy) to resell AT&T service at a discount. They were, to use an obvious pun, a bunch of high-flyers. Sloppy business practices and incomplete records were abundant. Coming from a staid telephone utility background, I was somewhat of a stuffed shirt; but what I found at US Telephone would have curled most people's toes.

One of my first assignments was to travel to Dallas to meet with and cancel the very expensive arrangements of a number of contractors. One carried a gun (which seemed to have nothing to do with his function as a building contractor), and he was not reluctant to display it for me as I terminated his retainer. Another was a very attractive young lady (a former Braniff flight attendant) who was apparently and handsomely paid to hang around and thereby "decorate" the office.

They were a wild bunch that didn't have much reverence for the rules. I remember shortly before we closed the acquisition, we received an urgent notice that the FCC was revoking US Telephone's domestic license to operate. They had elected a foreign national (Mexican, I recall) to their Board of Directors (despite a provision in our acquisition agreement not to make any such management or other changes prior to closing), in direct contravention of the FCC's rules (which required prior regulatory approval). We had to scramble to get that Director's resignation and appease the FCC, so we wouldn't have to shut down all U.S. operations. That incident brought home to me that I was no longer in the cozy world of the old telephone business where decades of precedent controlled almost every move. I had to learn to be more fleet afoot.

One of the bright lights at US Telephone, though, was Alan Stewart. He was a lawyer (formerly in the Legal Department at Braniff) with a great deal of integrity. He helped me through the maze in Dallas to root out the problems and mischief, and he came to Kansas City as my chief legal aide. He and his lovely wife, Cappy, were good friends, and I miss them both. There were a handful of other good people from US Telephone that came to Kansas City, like Sharon Jenkins (who helped establish Sprint's marketing program, and then moved on to bigger and better positions in the industry) and Shea Odum (who got married, is raising a family and still works for Sprint). But otherwise there are only a few remnants of US Telephone left.

Fiber Optic Network (FON)

While we were trying to straighten out the problems at US Telephone, Bill Esrey feverishly pushed a group of bright, young strategic planners that he had assembled in Kansas City to create a more cohesive vision of the future. Under Bill's direction, they resolved that competition against the giant AT&T could succeed if the company seized a technological and cost advantage by constructing the nation's first all-digital, fiber optic long distance network. It was ambitious and risky, but the business plan was well thought out, tested and credible. Bill announced the plan to shareholders at the April 1984 annual meeting, and the work began. The first construction began along the Chicago-to-St. Louis route, and very quickly US Telecom became the largest single purchaser of fiber optic cable in the world.

The strategic decision had been made to utilize railroad rights-of-way, and one of my first assignments at US Telecom was to complete the negotiations for nationwide access. The team (people like John Lucas, Wood Kinnard and Kevin Rucker) had made great progress; but there was a huge void in the Southeast United States, where the CSX Railroad had a virtual monopoly. CSX had entered into a joint venture with Southern New England Telephone (SNET), called Lightnet, to lease fiber optic capacity; but we wanted to own (not lease) our facilities.

So, we (mostly Bill McDonald and me) entered into months of negotiations with CSX's attorneys (Arnold & Porter) in Washington, D.C. We frequently reported our progress to Bill Esrey, who repeatedly set ever-higher objectives for us. I remember thinking at the time that Esrey would have a difficult time buying a used car (since every time the salesman agreed to Bill's offer, he'd lower it).

When we finally reached an acceptable deal, CSX treated us to a celebratory weekend at the Greenbriar resort (which CSX owned) in West Virginia. The subsequent relationship, though, was marred by disputes and some litigation.

In any event, construction of the first all-digital, 23,000-mile nationwide fiber optic telecommunications network in less than three years was heralded as one of the greatest accomplishments of the post-war era. It is not an overstatement (in my view) to say that Sprint's network launched a new era of information technology. But it is a story of people, as much as technology. The scale and complexity of the construction was unprecedented, and it took literally thousands of dedicated people working endless hours, often overcoming enormous obstacles with creative solutions.

For instance, the company's engineers had to design and build a huge circular saw containing more than 100 carbide-tipped steel teeth that sat on a railroad car to cut an 18-inch deep trench through limestone-silicate rock in the Feather River Canyon in northern California. Normal construction averaged about 75 miles per day;

but the 75 miles in the Feather River Canyon, using the new machine (called "Jaws"), took more than a year and cost $15 million. At the other end of the spectrum was Buck, the horse, who was used to haul reels of fiber optic cable over the Berkshire Mountains (between Albany, NY and Springfield, MA) during the winter of 1985.

And the cost was stunning; at the height of construction, the company spent a billion dollars more than the reseller operations produced (it put in perspective, at least for me, Lee Iacocca's pleas for a Congressional bail-out of Chrysler in 1979). I distinctly recall a meeting in 1987 when Bill McDonald, who headed the company's network construction efforts, reminded his troops that by lunchtime every day that year they'd cost the company about $10 million. The magnitude of the undertaking was almost unfathomable and caused many sleepless nights.

AT&T didn't help the situation by publicly laughing out loud, proclaiming that our plans were "folly" because their copper wire network was fully adequate to handle all of the world's telecommunications traffic for decades to come. AT&T eventually had to eat those words, specifically writing off almost their entire investment (about $17 billion, much more than the net worth of our whole company at the time) over the next few years to recognize technological obsolescence and finance fiber optic replacements. AT&T, in many respects, has been following the leader ever since. And that isn't just my opinion; I recall with great fondness an article in the July 31, 1989 issue of *BusinessWeek* magazine, entitled "People Aren't Laughing At US Sprint Anymore: The No. 3 Long-Distance Carrier Is Taking Business From AT&T and Challenging MCI," which included quotes such as "Sprint has gone from a laughing stock to a force to be reckoned with."

Bill Esrey's strategy always included attracting a partner to share the financial burden and competitive risk of building a nationwide competitive network. And, in his usual style, Esrey went about finding such a partner in a calculated and thorough manner. He retained an investment banker (First Boston), compiled a comprehensive prospectus, and went "on the road" to sell the story (on a confidential basis) to dozens of large companies in several different industries (including, for instance, automobile manufacturers and oil companies) who had the inclination and resources to participate. I participated in a few of these "road shows" and, in the course thereof, persuaded myself that, despite the risk and enormous expense, building the network was a brilliant strategy. The effort did not produce a financial partner, but led us to the deal with GTE.

AT&T Divestiture

The turmoil of those times was aided and abetted by the AT&T divestiture. The long distance market, over the objections of both the incumbent telephone industry and regulators, was opened to competition by MCI litigation in 1974.

The fact is that technology made it inevitable. Microwave technology was first used extensively by the military in World War II (because the army was more mobile than during WWI, when they strung coils of wire between trenches). After the war, companies with multiple fixed locations (and the need for extensive communications between those locations) built private microwave networks to improve communications paths and control costs.

Soon, independent contractors were building those networks for private companies and yearned to offer excess capacity to the public. That made them "common carriers" under prevailing regulatory law, but the FCC declined to license them as competitors against the incumbent monopoly. The courts, however, found no good reason to restrain innovation and authorized MCI (which became known, during those litigious years, as a law firm with a microwave antenna on the roof) to enter the market.

Despite those court rulings, though, AT&T continued to fight the onslaught of competition. The result was that, at one time during the early 1980s, AT&T was the defendant in over five dozen private antitrust cases. The U.S. Justice Department also brought an antitrust case against AT&T, alleging AT&T was using its local monopoly telephone operations to harm companies trying to enter the competitive long distance marketplace (by providing inferior or delayed local connections, or raising the costs of those connections, or all of the above).

At the time, AT&T was the largest, most successful and certainly most politically powerful private company in the world, and it was unfathomable (at least to me) that the government could prevail in this lawsuit. But U.S. District Court Judge Harold Greene (who, sadly, passed away at 76, on January 29, 2000) saw it differently. At the close of the government's evidence in the trial, he issued an opinion saying, essentially, that the case against AT&T had been proven and AT&T had almost impossible hurdles to overcome in order to avoid losing on all issues. Based thereon, the trial was recessed and AT&T entered serious settlement negotiations with the Department of Justice ("DOJ"), which resulted in the announcement in January 1982 (interestingly, on the same day the DOJ announced the dismissal of the IBM antitrust suit) of a Consent Decree that would break up the old Bell System on January 1, 1984.

The impact of the news was stunning. There had been much speculation during the settlement negotiations that AT&T was going to have to give up one or two of the Bell Operating Companies (BOCs) to satisfy the government, but hardly anyone forecast total divestiture. Indeed, I recall writing a memo to United Telecom's President (Ray Alden) opining that, because total divestiture was so radical and potentially harmful to the way telephone service had been provided in this country from the beginning, the government was sure to come to its senses and reduce the remedy before it could be implemented. It was not the first, or last, time that I was wrong; but it taught me the invaluable lesson that looking forward (rather than backward) was critical in a changing environment.

The good news for US Telecom's fiber optic network strategy was that the divestiture Decree created the concept of LATAs (local access and transport areas) to distinguish between the BOCs' local monopoly territories and competitive long distance service. At the time, there were 22 BOCs, but they were combined into seven Regional BOCs (or RBOCs), being:

RBOC	**BOCs**	**States**	**Assets**	**Revenues (6/30/83)**
Ameritech	Ill. Bell	Illinois	$ 16.26 B	$ 8.90 Billion
	Ind. Bell	Indiana		
	Mich. Bell	Michigan		
	Ohio Bell	Ohio		
	Wisc. Bell	Wisconsin		
Bell Atlantic	NJ Bell	New Jersey	$ 16.26 B	$ 8.73 Billion
	Bell of PA	Pennsylvania		
	C&P of Md	Maryland		
	C&P of Va	Virginia		
	C&P of WV	West Virginia		
	Diamond State	Delaware		
	C&P	District of Columbia		

BellSouth	South Central Southern Bell	Alabama Florida Georgia Kentucky Louisiana Mississippi North Carolina South Carolina Tennessee	$20.81 B	$ 10.51 Billion
NYNEX	NY Tel New England Tel	New York Connecticut Massachusetts Maine New Hampshire Rhode Island Vermont	$ 17.39 B	$ 10.01 Billion
Pacific Tel	Pacific Bell Nevada Bell	California Nevada	$ 16.19 B	$ 7.89 Billion
SBC	SW Bell	Arkansas Kansas Missouri Oklahoma Texas	$ 15.51 B	$ 7.86 Billion
US West	Mountain States NW Bell Pacific NW Bell	Arizona Colorado Idaho Iowa Minnesota Montana Nebraska New Mexico North Dakota South Dakota Oregon Utah Washington Wyoming	$ 15.05 B	$ 7.59 Billion

The RBOCs were required to allow long distance competitors to establish one or more Points of Presence (or POPs) in each LATA to establish connections to local customers. That enabled US Telecom to design its fiber optic network so that it could have access to every customer in the country by connecting to, initially, just one point in each of (initially) 126 LATAs (rather than having to run facilities to every one of over 2,000 communities nationwide). It was an extremely helpful development that enabled US Telecom, both economically and technologically, to provide service everywhere in the U.S., not just in large cities.

Stockholders

The April 1984 Annual Shareholders meeting also, by the way, marked the end of decades of continuous annual increases in the dividends paid to holders of United Telecom's common stock. That event signaled a major change in the nature of United Telecom stock from an income investment to a riskier growth opportunity, and the market reacted accordingly. During the next few years (while the fiber optic network was being built), an enormous amount of United Telecom stock changed hands as the "little old ladies in tennis shoes" sought safer investments and the speculators moved in.

It was not a time for the timid as the stock price — which used to move only fractions of a point, if at all, each month — started to fluctuate one or more points each trading day. The risk eventually paid off handsomely for stockholders; but the tough transition provides an example of what publicly held local telephone companies can expect as they enter the competitive fray in their markets.

CHAPTER THREE

US Sprint

THE TASK OF PROVIDING facilities-based competitive long distance service was daunting, both financially and operationally. At the time, no one (except, of course, AT&T) was doing it very well or profitably. The second (to MCI) largest competitor to AT&T was GTE Sprint. That company began when Southern Pacific Railroad decided to resell some of its microwave capacity along railroad tracks (that it used primarily to communicate with trains) to the public. It formed a subsidiary (Southern Pacific Communications) and named the service Sprint (there is to this day a persistent but unproven rumor that the name was an acronym, which stood for Southern Pacific Railroad Internal Network for Telecommunications). SP eventually tired of the losses and sold SP Communications to GTE (which re-named the company GTE Sprint).

ENFIA Tariffs

At the time, there was a mammoth regulatory dispute over the charges to be paid by competitors to connect to the BOCs' local telephone networks. The BOCs had, naturally, engineered their local networks to provide connections to only one (AT&T's) long distance network. Thus, competitors (like US Telecom and GTE Sprint) had to connect much like any other retail customer; that is, they had to order local service (a seven-digit number) and provide their long distance dial-tone to customers who called (who then had to enter the number they were calling, plus a personal identification number or PIN so they could be billed).

The result was customers of competitors had to dial as many as 22 digits to complete a long distance call, whereas AT&T's customers could dial only ten digits (1+area code+local number). Competitors argued that this dialing disadvantage, in addition to the diminished circuit quality (because the calls had to go through extra switching), constituted an inferior grade of service for which they should receive a discount. In particular, they wanted to pay the BOCs far less than AT&T paid for its superior connections to the BOCs' local networks. The dispute was further complicated by the fact that the charges paid by AT&T were not based on costs (primarily because, having been integrated for a century and not having to separate those costs, neither AT&T nor the BOCs really knew precisely what the incremental costs of connections were). The BOCs, on the other hand, argued that any discount would constitute an unjustified subsidy to competitors.

The regulators, faced with this difficult and complex dispute, exercised their normal amount of courage and declined to rule. Instead, the FCC hosted meetings of the combatants and encouraged them to reach a negotiated settlement. The result, after months of bitter talks, was an agreement whereby the BOCs would initially charge competitors 35% of the connection price paid by AT&T for a period of time, which would then be increased to 45% for a time, then increased finally to 55%. These terms were incorporated into a federal tariff (called Exchange Network Facilities for Interconnection Arrangements, or ENFIA) which was filed with and approved by the FCC.

GTE Sprint

Some industry planners, especially those at GTE, reportedly assumed that some access price discount would continue at least until competitors achieved profitability. Indeed, GTE commissioned a study by Booz, Allen & Hamilton and presented it to the FCC, which concluded that long distance competition could not survive without a permanent discount in the price for local connections. It was not the first or last time in my experience that a consultant was woefully wrong.

The AT&T divestiture required, among other things, that the BOCs should provide "equal access" to competitors (that is, they should re-engineer or replace their local switches within certain time periods to provide the same type of 1+ connections to competitors that AT&T enjoyed) at cost-based rates. As the BOCs implemented this requirement (Independent local telephone companies were ordered by the FCC to do likewise, but over a longer period of time), the ENFIA discounts went away and GTE lost its appetite for the long distance market.

As an aside, I remember the United Telephone System's reaction to this development with some chagrin. President Bob Snedaker demanded that the UTS companies comply with the mandate to convert local switching to equal access, but also insisted that they carefully develop access charges (which would replace the old method of "separations and settlements" with AT&T) so that long distance revenues would not suffer. He gathered all of the UTS rate planners at a hotel near the KCI airport on February 3, 1983, and admonished them to err, if at all, on the side of a revenue increase. George Fuciu (who had been hired by Art Krause, and later went on to a distinguished career in UTS and as head of long distance network operations for Sprint) was put in charge, and his team did an incredible job of producing UTS's federal and state access charge tariffs in a timely and very profitable manner. The problem is that the BOCs followed the same strategy and developed access rates that were far above actual costs which, especially as long distance traffic volumes increased, produced record earnings for them (at the expense of long distance competitors) for years to come.

In any event, during July 1985, Paul Henson and Ted Brophy, then Chairman of GTE, talked about a possible joint venture between GTE Sprint and US Telecom. Secret task forces were formed between the two companies to determine the feasibility of a deal. GTE had to agree to, basically, throw away over a billion dollars in microwave assets and adopt US Telecom's fiber optic network strategy.

As an aside, the company later used GTE's write-off of the microwave assets in a TV commercial. Although those assets were, in reality, mostly disassembled and resold, we videotaped one tower being blown up with dynamite. It made for some dramatic footage, which was used to demonstrate the passing of the old technology (much to MCI's consternation). Although the TV ad didn't sell much long distance service (and, therefore, wasn't run for very long), it did make an impact on regulators, some of whom thereafter repeatedly referred to it as an example of advancing technology.

In any event, by Thanksgiving of 1985, the decision had been made to form a 50/50 partnership, and both GTE and United Telecom sent their lawyers to GTE's training facility in Norwalk, Connecticut (which was closed to give us privacy) to negotiate a definitive agreement. A small group of us worked literally day and night in seclusion until after Christmas to complete the agreements.

On January 16, 1986 the deal was publicly announced. The officers of both companies met (some for the first time) at an airport hotel in Atlanta on January 17-18, to celebrate the deal and begin planning the future. Then the real work began.

Regulatory Approvals

I had the responsibility of obtaining needed regulatory approvals from the state public service commissions (PSCs), the FCC and the DOJ. The DOJ was the first and the toughest. We had essentially two problems to overcome. Even though each company had only a minuscule market share, we were putting together the number two and three competitors to AT&T. The DOJ was concerned about the fact that we were eliminating customer choice. Our argument was that we needed the economies of size that would result in order to compete against the dominant AT&T.

More troubling was the fact that GTE, when it acquired SP Communications, had agreed to a Consent Decree which did not require the divestiture of GTE local telephone operations, but mandated strict separation between them and the competitive long distance business. The DOJ had declined to impose similar restrictions on US Telecom (when we acquired US Telephone), and we were not interested in having them imposed on Sprint. After extensive discovery and negotiations with the DOJ, they eventually conceded and approved our deal.

At the same time our folks were exerting super-human efforts to complete the remaining regulatory approvals, which required some folks to literally spend days and nights on airplanes to meet with regulators across the nation. (I remember, in particular, approving an expense report for Sheryl Wright — a very special young lady who did remarkable work for the company from the day she was hired — that included airline flights to four cities over two days, but no hotel bill). Our target was July 1, and we barely made it. I remember being in the San Francisco airport on June 27, getting the message from my staff that all approvals were secure, and cheerfully calling Charles Skibo to give him the good news.

Putting It Together

The rest of the company was working equally hard to prepare to combine the operations — networks, sales, marketing, finance, data processing (especially billing), human resources, etc. — by July 1. The department heads of both companies met monthly in

Scottsdale, Arizona (halfway between Kansas City and San Francisco, the headquarters of GTE Sprint) to review progress. Those were fascinating meetings, not only because of the personal dynamics of people who used to be bitter competitors, but especially because of the remarkable creativity that resulted.

Many of the people from both US Telecom and GTE Sprint had learned the business from the local telephone operations of their respective parent companies, and had yet to master the art of competition. Indeed, in our immature way, many of us thought that in order to be successful we had to be loud, arrogant and aggressive. We thought that hating our competitors was expected; so working together was incomprehensible. But we soon came to realize that the real enemy wasn't us (but was AT&T), and that the way to win was to please customers (instead of fighting MCI, AT&T and other competitors). It took awhile but, when we came together, we became a force to be reckoned with.

Everyone, with few exceptions, worked hard to launch the joint venture in a timely and effective manner. I do recall, however, the shock that many felt when the Human Relations folks announced that they couldn't put all the necessary HR systems in place in time, so that the partners would have to separately employ the partnership employees for an additional six months or so. I give the tri-CEOs (Skibo, Prigmore & Hann) credit for not publicly criticizing the HR folks, but taking them aside and making sure they delivered on time.

A more fond recollection of those times pertained to advertising. US Telecom had used Foote, Cone & Belding, and GTE Sprint had used J. Walter Thompson, as their advertising agencies. In an effort to be fair in the choice between the two, it was decided to allow both to make presentations to one of the Scottsdale meetings on the advertising campaigns they would recommend for the new partnership (which was subsequently named US Sprint). J. Walter Thompson clearly did the best job and was selected.

But, in their presentation, J. Walter Thompson proposed three TV ads. One was a comparison of the old rock-and-roll song "Don't Hang Up" on a 45 rpm record (representing the old AT&T technology) and on a compact disc (representing the digital fiber optic quality of US Sprint). I really liked that one (probably because I liked the old song); but AT&T threatened to sue us because they thought it was derogatory. AT&T never had much of a sense of humor. Another ad pictured a phone call placed from a rural phone booth by a dusty cowboy to an attractive urbane young lady in a modern downtown condo. It was appealing, but it didn't sell much long distance service.

The third ad was a group of engineers listening to a pin drop over a US Sprint fiber optic line (with one of them asking "That was a pin?"). I hated that one, because the pin drop was taken from an old hackneyed expression which didn't (I believed) reflect the exciting technology of our new company. The marketers (thankfully) didn't listen to me, and the pin drop came to be one of the most successful advertising signatures in the industry's history. I (and everyone else) learned that I should stay out of marketing decisions.

Billing Problems

In any event, US Sprint was successfully launched on July 1, 1986. It was a great day, but we were soon to be the victims of our own success. One of the most creative decisions made in the early days was the Charter Customer Offer, which gave customers who signed up for US Sprint service a 10% discount off their long distance bills for a year. It seems rather modest in these current days of seemingly never-ending promotions, but it was the first "sale" of long distance service ever in the industry. Regulators were reluctant to approve such blasphemy, but customers loved it. In fact, as I recall, we forecast that the offer would generate about 400,000 new customers in six months; but almost a million more customers flocked to US Sprint. The bad news is that we were not well prepared for the influx.

Specifically, we had decided to use the old US Telecom billing system, which could not handle the volume of customers that the Charter Customer Offer produced. Moreover, our data clerks were ill prepared to enter new customers into the system at the rate of almost 20 every minute of every business day for six months. Mistakes were made, and we suffered from the old adage of "garbage-in, garbage-out." Billing records were a mess and, as a result, when we issued bills, they were often in error. Customers were infuriated (even though many got no bills and, therefore, free service). Competitors delighted in our troubles (MCI's founder, Bill McGowan, liked to call us "Splint"), and state regulators and attorneys general commenced investigations. The FCC issued a stinging show cause order, demanding that the problems be fixed.

No one wanted to correct the problems more than we did, but

(as the head of our data processing department said at the time) it was like trying to change a flat tire on a car going 60 miles per hour. It was painful, but we finally fixed the problems with an entirely new billing system (that quickly became another competitive advantage). The bad reputation lingered for a couple of years, though. I learned that in a competitive environment when you do something nice for a customer, he or she will think well of you for a few minutes; but if you offend customers, they will remember it for years to come.

Management Changes

In addition, during these early years we added to the chaos with a number of management changes. US Sprint started with an Office of the President, consisting of the three presidents of the combined entities — being Charles Skibo (US Telecom), Don Prigmore (GTE Sprint) and David Hann (GTE Telenet). Don left soon after the partnership began in mid-1986, and Charles and David split the governing responsibilities. Charles oversaw sales and operations, and David handled data and administrative functions (so David was my boss for a time). David left after a while, though, to pursue more entrepreneurial opportunities. The last I heard, he was elected mayor of Paradise Valley, Arizona (which struck me as ironic, since he didn't seem to particularly like politics when I worked for him).

The concept of co-executives (especially co-CEOs) in mergers and acquisitions has become somewhat popular and controversial these days. They are often criticized as unworkable. I think they can work, but usually don't because of the egos of the people involved. That's not necessarily bad, because you want a CEO with enough of an ego to believe in his or her ability to lead the enterprise to bigger and better results. But the battle of egos can be disruptive.

Indeed, management disruption was the hallmark of US Sprint's early years. Skibo was a great salesman and was primarily responsible for recruiting marketing talent and infusing a genuine sense of competition in the workforce. His legacy is that he built Sprint's customer base to five million in one year. But administration was not his strong suit; which caused problems at a time when the company desperately needed discipline and, consequently, he departed in mid-1987.

Bob Snedaker, who had been President of the United Telephone

System (who brought me back to Kansas City from Tennessee in 1980), was named the new President of US Sprint. His competitive credentials were questionable, but it was generally believed that Bob's appointment was a concession to GTE's President Rocky Johnson (who was a career local telephone man and long-time friend of Bob's), since he and Esrey were not believed (as a result of their competition for Paul's job) to be close associates. Bob was a strong manager, and he focused on correcting many of the company's problems (especially the billing fiasco). He knocked heads and didn't make many friends, but he got the job done.

Regardless, when United Telecom took over management control of US Sprint in July 1988, Snedaker was out and Esrey named himself to head the enterprise. He presided over the conversion of the company to profitability in late 1988, and a year later turned the reins over to Ron LeMay. Ron served as President of Sprint's long distance division until 1995, when (Ron became President and COO of the parent company and) Gary Forsee succeeded him. Forsee served until 1998 (when he became CEO of Global One), and Patti Manuel became long distance President. Patti left the company in 1999, and Ron LeMay announced that the position would be eliminated.

Thus, in its 13-year history, Sprint long distance operations had no less than six Presidents. And that office reflected stability compared to some others. There was a period of five years (1984-89) when I had eight bosses (Krause, Esrey, Skibo, Hann, Currey, Fuller, LeMay and Devlin). It was both personally and professionally disconcerting. The greatest evil of such turnover, in my view, is that people tend not to make a commitment to their boss (and, therefore, the direction they're given to do their jobs) because of the likelihood that he or she will soon be replaced by someone else with different priorities, objectives and style.

For that reason, I was very stubborn about making organizational changes to my department (with one exception). Goodness knows that circumstances (i.e., reorganizations and realignments in the rest of the company) dictated change, but I tried very hard to minimize the impact on my group. I wanted to inject some stability so the folks would stay focused on the difficult job of maintaining the company's state and federal government relations. The result was that I had some very good people in jobs for which they were not the best suited, but I hoped they could overcome the challenges and do their jobs if they were insulated from the kind of management turmoil that I was experiencing.

Public Relations
The exception was Public Relations. In 1988, the person Charles Skibo had brought in to bolster US Sprint's P.R. program left the company, and I was asked to try to get the function under control. The department had a $3 million annual budget, but was spending at almost three times that rate. I had to downsize and bring some fiscal discipline to the group. And all of this had to be done at a time — such as Sprint's winning a share of the FTS-2000 contract — when P.R. was important to the company.

With the help of some good people, like Bill Musgrave (who was VP, but later left to head KC's Science City project) and Roseanne Palmisano (who faithfully, accurately and constantly crunched the numbers), we got the job done in nine months. It was a challenging assignment, but I was glad to turn it over to a P.R. professional (when Ron LeMay hired Jerry Cosley away from TWA; he's now with UtiliCorp United).

One of my memories of those days was when *Forbes Magazine* invited us (Charles Skibo, me and a couple others) to lunch at their headquarters on Fifth Avenue in New York City. They wanted to discuss some of the issues facing competitive long distance carriers, and to solicit some of our advertising business. After Kip Forbes gave us a tour of their private museum and offices, we ate and talked with him and Steve Forbes, as well as several editors and reporters. It was an impressive afternoon, and I remain today a big fan of the Forbes family.

Operational Challenges
US Sprint, although not exactly a "start-up" company, faced many of the same challenges. Indeed, the entire competitive long distance industry was in those early days besieged by less-than-honest entrepreneurs looking to take advantage of our inexperience. Before the days of equal access, when customers of competitive carriers had to dial multi-digit access codes, the crooks figured out how (using computers) to randomly replicate those codes and thereby steal long distance service from legitimate customers. It quickly and unfortunately became a multi-million-dollar problem.

We could make the codes unbreakable by making them longer, but longer codes were not attractive to the legitimate customers (who did not want to stand at payphones dialing two dozen or more digits). So, we devised "code abuse" programs to detect when unauthorized users were on the system; we tracked them down and aggressively prosecuted them. Those programs eventually allowed us to control the problem, but it wasn't eliminated until 1+ dialing was fully implemented.

We also suffered from the costs of access. Access charges to local telephone companies for connections to our long distance customers were frightfully high, representing about half the cost of each call (even though we were paying for only the "first-and-last mile" of cross-country transmissions). Moreover, local telephone companies felt no obligation to help competitive long distance companies efficiently manage their access arrangements (even though we were among their largest customers, in dollars paid). So US Sprint put together a group (called the Line Costs Task Force) to attack the problem.

I was asked to head the group, but the work was really done by folks like Mont Williams (who subsequently went to work for Ameritech), Deb Keating (who's still making a contribution at Sprint) and Rich Nespola (who left to start a very successful telecommunications consulting firm). Over several months of intensive research and negotiations with the BOCs, we accomplished millions in savings. And we established priorities and procedures which (were subsequently improved by our successors and have become routine today) that enable Sprint to have some of the lowest percentage access costs in the industry.

The industry still hasn't made one of the changes that I advocated, though. One of the big problems, in my view, is that access charges are applied by local telephone companies to each minute of use of their facilities by long distance carriers. This is a holdover, I believe, from the traditional method of charging per-minute for long distance service; but it makes no sense (and, indeed, is probably detrimental) in today's circumstances. Competition caused long distance usage to increase by double-digit annual percentages, and the industry now processes billions of long distance minutes each month. Thus, billing for access on a per-minute basis is (as I said in a speech to the 1988 Winter Meeting of the National Association of Regulatory Utility Commissioners, or "NARUC") akin to buying a truck-load of sand one grain at a time.

It is extremely inefficient, in particular, when you consider that the cost of tracking and billing for each minute probably exceeds (and unnecessarily increases) the costs of providing the underlying service. Accordingly, I advocated a number of short and long-term solutions, including bulk billing, longer payment periods and distance-insensitive charges. I'd hoped that those ideas had gained some traction when *Telematics* (a now defunct industry journal) published my remarks (edited by Ron Havens) in the April 1988 issue (Vol. 5, No. 4), but nothing meaningful came of it.

CompTel

The creation of US Sprint propelled us into the forefront of the rather nascent competitive long distance industry segment. MCI had been around for a decade, but they reveled in their image as rebels and usually didn't join with their colleagues in any meaningful industry efforts. Both GTE Sprint and US Telecom had been members of a start-up association of alternative long distance carriers, which asked US Sprint to take the lead in bringing it to maturity. They changed the name to the Competitive Telecommunications Association ("CompTel"), and I was elected Chairman (I served two terms, from March 1986 to 1988).

The Board of Directors worked hard to establish credibility, and I think the association made real progress in representing the interests of long distance competitors in federal forums. Over the years, as Sprint grew, our interests came to conflict in some cases with those of the smaller members of CompTel, and we withdrew from formal membership; but Sprint still stayed closely aligned with many of their goals. Today CompTel is headed by Russell Frisby, a former Chairman of the Maryland PSC, and is a very professional and effective group.

Quality Program

Bill Esrey (and many others in senior management) was deeply troubled with the sloppy business practices that resulted from the turmoil of the times. So Bill spearheaded the Quality movement at Sprint. He personally researched Quality programs at other successful companies, and developed a modified approach that he believed would work best at Sprint. It was focused on fact-based decision making, a disciplined approach to problem-solving, and respect for fellow employees. Many were skeptical that it was the management fad-of-the-month, but everyone underwent training and it was implemented company-wide.

The principles of Sprint Quality were very basic, and it clearly contributed to the turnaround of the company. The greatest benefit, it seemed to me, was that it established a basic set of rules that everyone willingly and proudly followed.

Unfortunately, after a few years an internal Quality bureaucracy developed and normal turnover resulted in many new employees who've not had extensive training. It's a good program, but many employees today seem to lack real enthusiasm for the rigors of Quality.

I do not have the same respect for many other management programs, though. In fact, over the years I became quite disillusioned with both some management training and some of the people who claim to have benefited therefrom. Good managers, it seems to me, develop over time through their business experience and relationships with their subordinates, peers and superiors. If they have to be taught by outsiders the basics of human nature, then their personal development is likely too deficient for them to ever understand how to effectively motivate and manage people. Worse are those management training programs that promote gimmicks for dealing with people (usually requiring the trainee to buy the trainer's new book) and the erstwhile managers that adopt those gimmicks without any independent thought or evaluation of their usefulness or application.

The Numbers

A summary of the story of US Sprint can be found, I believe, in the numbers. The losses incurred by US Sprint were enormous, totaling almost $1.8 billion, and unprecedented in an industry that was accustomed to assured rates of return. Quarter-by-quarter, the numbers were:

Quarter	Losses (millions)
3Q86	($159)
4Q86	($198)
1Q87	($241)
2Q87	($633)
3Q87	($165)
4Q87	($116)
1Q88	($138)
2Q88	($112)
3Q88	($ 19)

The impact on the company's stock was dramatic. A few shareholders believed in the strategy and stuck with the company during the lean years, and it has certainly paid off for those who did (having split two-for-one in January 1990 and again in June 1999). A CEO's focus should always be primarily upon providing a return for stockholders, and Bill Esrey — whether or not he has a winning personality — has unquestionably fulfilled that responsibility. The question, especially in the context of the pending merger with MCI/WorldCom, is whether that responsibility should be fulfilled in the short term or the long term, considering the impact upon Sprint's employees (and their families) and the community. I'll explore that discussion a little more later.

CHAPTER FOUR

Sprint Corp.

NINETEEN-HUNDRED AND EIGHTY-EIGHT was the year it all, finally, came together for Sprint. Construction of the nationwide fiber optic network was substantially completed, the billing and other operational problems were behind us, and the long distance business turned profitable for the first time. As I recall, August was our first profitable month. The fact that we were in the black was kept secret from most employees, because (after the years of oppressive losses) it seemed too good to be true. We came close in the third quarter, but it was not until we publicly announced the fourth quarter financial results that everyone knew we had made it.

I remember that year the NCAA Final Four Tournament was held at Kemper Arena in Kansas City and, remarkably, two Big Eight (now the Big Twelve) teams (Kansas and Oklahoma) played in the championship game. (As an MU fan, it's tough for me to admit, but KU won — led by Danny Manning). We hosted Senator Jack Danforth in the company's suite at that game. He was normally a reserved gentleman, but a great basketball fan. He kept asking me how the company was doing; I tried to restrain my enthusiasm for how close we were, finally, to a breakthrough.

GTE Sells Out

Despite the fact that we were clearly on the path to profitability, GTE never seemed to get excited about its investment in US Sprint. GTE ran its considerable local telephone operations in a gentlemanly manner, and I don't think they ever got comfortable with the dog-eat-dog mentality in the competitive long distance marketplace. So it was with little regret that GTE agreed to sell its 50% partnership interest in US Sprint to United Telecom.

The story of how the deal was reached is rather quaint. Paul Henson and Bill Esrey had been talking with GTE's Chairman, Ted Brophy, and President, Rocky Johnson, about selling out for some time. They plotted to try to close the deal on the golf course. Bill and Rocky played in a twosome ahead of Paul and Ted. Well into the match, Rocky agreed to Bill's terms. To alert Paul to his success, Bill wrote a short note on a scrap of paper and left it on the ball-washer. When Paul got to that hole, he picked up the note, read it, smiled to himself and put it in his pocket (and subsequently had it framed and hung in his office). It's a classic story of how important golf can be to big business. Unfortunately, I never liked the game. It never made sense to me that a two-inch putt counts the same as a 200-yard drive. Perhaps my career suffered as a result.

In any event, the deal provided that United Telecom became the managing partner of US Sprint and took full management control. In 1989, Bill Esrey reorganized both United Telecom and US Sprint to reflect that control and position the company for the future. In 1992, United Telecom completed the purchase of GTE's interest and changed the name of the parent company (as well as the long distance division) to Sprint Corp.

There were some reservations in the United Telephone System to the name change; they felt some historical bond to the old name and didn't want to change. Even though I'd spent a decade working in UTS, that attitude surprised me. United Telecom and UTS were never household names, and we were investing about $100 million a year in advertising to build the Sprint brand. Most people have now come to understand that the nationwide brand is one of the company's most valuable assets.

FTS-2000

Also it was the year 1988 that Sprint won 40% of the FTS-2000 contract. AT&T had historically been the sole source provider of telecommunications services to federal government agencies. But, with the advent of equal access in the mid-1980s, the General Services Administration (or GSA, the government's landlord) decided to procure long distance service on a competitive basis and thereby achieve savings for the agencies and taxpayers. Because it had never been done before, the GSA decided to issue proposed procurements for public comment, before actually soliciting bids. This process of trial-and-error took a couple of years to play out, and produced a number of important changes and corrections to the procurement, which ultimately led to its overwhelming success.

For instance, one of the early proposals required bidders to provide, in addition to normal long distance, 800 service (or toll-free calling) to the government. At the time, AT&T owned and operated the 800 number database, so customers who wanted to buy 800 service from a competitor had to agree to change their existing 800 numbers (which was a significant impediment, since many users were reluctant to change their affinity numbers — like 800-FLOWERS — and/or had widely published their 800 numbers in advertising, letterhead, business cards, etc.). Competitive long distance companies had to persuade the GSA not to require 800 service as a part of the FTS-2000 procurement until the FCC mandated a nationwide 800 database that enabled customers to keep their 800 numbers when they changed carriers.

Early versions of the proposed procurement also were structured in a way that dictated the prime bidder be a system integrator, and long distance companies were relegated to subcontractor status. During this period US Sprint sought to align with EDS, but the relationship was never satisfactory. In particular, EDS's view of who should do the work and who should reap most of the margins was incompatible with US Sprint's expectations. Congress got involved, though, and fixed the problem.

That's when I first got to know Jim Lewin, who was Chief Investigator for the House Government Operations Committee and a trusted staffer for Chairman Jack Brooks (D-TX). Brooks and Lewin were tough overseers of the GSA and were determined to make the FTS-2000 contract a model for successful competitive procurements by the government. They worked tirelessly to improve the bidding process (by, among other things, eliminating the need for system integrators, creating a dual-award and providing for ongoing competition during the 10-year life of the contract) and encouraged Sprint to participate (to make sure the contract wasn't defaulted to AT&T and MCI). Their efforts paid off; the contract resulted in substantial technological upgrades while ultimately saving the government billions of dollars over the term. But they never got (or sought, for that matter) the credit they richly deserved.

There was also a lot of intrigue around the bidding process, which led to some ugly speculation in the press. That is when I first met Leslie Cauley, who is now a prominent reporter for the *Wall Street Journal* (and a special friend). She taught me the invaluable lesson of sticking to basic facts and not trying to obfuscate the truth, when dealing with the press. Enormous sums of money were spent preparing the bids, and huge potential revenues (estimated by some to be $25 billion over 10 years) were at stake, which helped create an environment conducive to abuse and rife with rumors.

For instance, each bidder had to make an Operational Capabilities Demonstration (OCD) to show the GSA how they would provide the service, maintenance and billing if they won. Sprint built a center in its Atlanta offices for this purpose (which we later used for sales presentations), and there were reports of excesses by the contractors hired to do the work. There were also reports of espionage (some people allegedly overheard competitors taking about bid prices in a restaurant and improperly appropriated that information to their unfair advantage). But subsequent investigations found no actionable wrongdoing.

Regardless, it was announced on December 7 that we'd won the minority share (AT&T won 60%) of the FTS-2000 contract. I remember on that day Bill Esrey was on the company plane flying to Mexico City to try to finalize an operating agreement with Telmex. He could be contacted only via a short telex message (that simply said "we won"). He had to land and call back to Kansas City for the details. He quickly returned for an early morning nationwide video press conference the next day to celebrate. It was a heady time, but even then we didn't realize how much credibility that win (and the right to provide service to the White House, the Treasury Department, the Justice Department, and other government agencies) would give us with large corporate customers in the marketplace. We were "for real" and we never turned back.

MCI, a perennial sore loser, protested the award (and lost) and continued to object and try to pick off government business during the entire life of the contract (with only limited success). They were a pest, but I have to admit that their constant complaining kept the government on its toes. In fact, the lessons learned during the FTS-2000 contract were put to good use as the GSA formulated the proposed procurement for the follow-on contract (dubbed FTS-2001) for the next 10 years.

Sprint formed a separate group — the Government Services Division (GSD) — headquartered in Herndon, Virginia (outside Washington, D.C.) to administer the FTS-2000 contract. The Government Affairs group worked closely with GSD because they were both serving the same constituency, and there were some controversial moments. For instance, in 1991 the GSA determined that the 60/40 contract split was out of balance and proposed to transfer the Navy Department off the AT&T network onto Sprint's in order to equalize the shares. AT&T, which historically had all of the Department of Defense's business (and, we believed, was continuing to charge the old, higher rates to DOD for pre-FTS-2000 services), aggressively protested the move. The debate quickly escalated to Congress, and there were a series of contentious hearings that examined the GSA's management of the contract and Sprint's practices. It was not a fun time, and the Navy decision was never implemented.

My involvement in the process of trying to resolve these disputes resulted in me being named to *Federal Computer Week's* list of the "1992 Federal 100." It's an annual award to "recognize people for their ability to manage, to influence, to shape the government systems arena." Although he never admitted it, I always suspected that I got the award primarily because Jim Lewin was one of the judges that year. Other recipients that year, interestingly, included Senator Al Gore (D-TN), Rep. John Conyers (D-MI) and Rep. Frank Horton (R-NY), as well as some folks who became good friends, like John Gioia (CEO of Robbins-Gioia, Inc.), Don Upson (who was then a House staffer and is now Secretary of Technology in Virginia), and Chuck Wheeler (House Committee staff).

In any event, FTS-2001 was bid in the summer and awarded in December 1999. It recognized the changes in the competitive long distance market (as well as legislative changes made by the Republican-led Congress) and gave the winners a preferred position to bid on each agency's business (rather than awarding an exclusive right to serve). It initially sought competitive procurements for local telephone service as well. But the GSA eventually had to recognize that the BOCs had not opened their markets to genuine competition (even though that had been mandated by the Telecommunications Act of 1996), and it deferred until later. Sprint won a majority share, and MCI won the rest; AT&T lost and hasn't stopped protesting. It will take awhile to transition from FTS-2000 and fully implement FTS-2001, but it appears that the new arrangement will once again prove to be very beneficial to the government and taxpayers.

Republican Convention

Nineteen-hundred and eighty-eight was also the year that Sprint was designated the primary long distance company for the Republican National Convention in New Orleans. It was the first time in history that a carrier other than AT&T had won that honor, and the company acquitted itself well (in fact, well enough to also win the business of the subsequent Bush Campaign). It also provided us with an unparalleled Government Affairs opportunity, and we took advantage of it with a presence at almost every event.

We also hosted a large 24-hour hospitality room on the second floor of the headquarters hotel on the river, just down the street from the convention center (The Louisiana Superdome), which required special credentials for admittance. It was often populated by weary delegates and members of the press. I remember Senator Danforth meeting me there to tell us that he was not going to be the Vice President nominee. Shortly thereafter, we were sitting there watching through the picture window George Bush's boat dock (he had flown into the nearby military base and taken a boat to the convention landing), when CNN announced on the TV that Bush was going to name his VP candidate. The press folks scrambled down to the dock to record Dan Quayle's remarks. I was disappointed. I had hoped that either Danforth or Senator Nancy Kassebaum (R-KS) would be Bush's choice, but it was fun watching history unfold.

The Dime Lady

Nineteen hundred and eighty-eight was the year that Candice Bergen became Sprint's official spokesperson. How that came about is an interesting story. At the time, AT&T was using Cliff Robertson in its commercials. MCI was using ad hoc ads that generally poked fun at AT&T. We had not, since the days of US Telecom, used a celebrity in our ads, mostly because of the cost. Nevertheless, there was a feeling that our ads had lost some punch and a new approach was needed. So, J. Walter Thompson coordinated some internal research to determine what might work.

They interviewed many officers and employees to try to understand and establish the company's identity. They asked (what seemed like at the time to be silly) questions like "Do you think the company is more like a Ford or a Ferrari? Like Nordstrom's or K-Mart? Like George Bush or Bette Midler?" All of the input was evaluated, and a consensus emerged that the company was fun, exciting, fast-moving, somewhat irreverent and feminine in nature. In fact, many people used Candice (who was in the early years of the Murphy Brown show) as an example of what Sprint was like.

So the company approached Candice, who happened to be a Sprint customer but had never endorsed a product before. She liked the idea, and a long-term contract was soon negotiated. Shortly thereafter, Murphy Brown won the first of many Emmy awards; and when representatives of the company called to congratulate Candice, she allowed (with her tongue only partially in her cheek) that the contract renewal was going to cost a little more.

While she was expensive, Candice quickly became the "top" rated corporate spokesperson in America and over 10 years added immeasurably to Sprint's success. Indeed, Candice's reputation as the "Dime Lady," while great for Sprint, troubled her (given her long and distinguished career, she had obviously hoped to be remembered for more) and eventually led to the end of the relationship.

Following Candice's departure, Sprint also discontinued most of its long, remarkably prolific and unusually creative relationship with J. Walter Thompson. It now uses a variety of ad agencies and consultants for different mediums and offerings across the country. Although I did not work that closely with them, I have to admit that I miss the inspiration, fancy and fun that J. Walter Thompson brought to Sprint's ads. There's little question that much of Sprint's market prominence over the past decade is attributable to their Candice campaign.

Sprint was without a national spokesperson for a few years, but has now contracted with Sela Ward to do TV commercials (she has done voiceovers for Sprint for about a year) beginning in 2000. Ms. Ward is an accomplished and alluring actress (she won an Emmy for "Sisters" and is now starring in "Once and Again"), but she has big shoes to fill as Sprint's new spokesperson.

International Cable

Nineteen-hundred and eighty-nine was also the year that Sprint ventured into international cable ownership. Transatlantic and transpacific telecommunications cables had historically been constructed and primarily owned by AT&T (with tiny minority ownership percentages held by other users), but the law (along with the market) was changing. A group of private investors proposed to construct the world's first Private Trans Atlantic Telecommunications cable (called PTAT) and lease capacity at competitive prices to others. While they were underway, they ran into financing problems, which provided an opportunity for Sprint.

We started negotiations with the PTAT owners in January, and

Bill Esrey put together an alliance with Cable & Wireless (which was the contractor that was laying and would maintain the undersea cable) to market the services worldwide. It was a powerful and unprecedented concept, and service was launched in July to much fanfare. But due (I believe) to private agendas of some folks in both Sprint and C&W, the alliance never came close to its potential and eventually was dissolved. Nevertheless, PTAT was the first of many transatlantic fiber optic cables, and it still operates at full capacity.

An Impressive Growth Story

I believe the real success story of Sprint is found in the numbers. I went to law school so, among other reasons, I wouldn't have to work with numbers; but, in this case, they are remarkably revealing. Here's a snapshot of the company's growth the past two decades:

Year	Assets (billions)	Employees	Revenues (billions)
1980	$ 4.206	29,320	$ 1.753
1981	4.621	29,680	2.263
1982	4.754	29,309	2.419
1983	4.945	27,218	2.511
1984	5.441	27,639	2.856
1985	5.767	27,415	3.198
1986	6.379	23,245	3.059
1987	6.558	23,325	2.982
1988	9.817	37,661	6.493
1989	9.821	41,400	7.549
1990	10.553	43,100	8.345
1991	10.464	43,200	8.780
1992	10.188	43,400	9.239
1993	14.149	50,000	11.368
1994	14.936	48,826	12.662
1995	15.196	48,265	12.765
1996	15.665	48,024	13.888
1997	16.581	50,600	14.874
1998	18.983	64,900	15.764
1999	21.969	71,000	17.016

These growth rates, I submit, are impressive. In less than two decades, we increased revenues more than eight-fold, increased assets by four and a half times, and more than doubled the number of very productive employees. Admittedly, these numbers do not compare to some of the dramatic results by some Internet-related and other high-tech companies that seem to have captured the fascination of the stock markets these days, but they are solid, were honestly and diligently achieved, and stand the test of time.

In the days when Sprint's earnings were lackluster (especially after the second quarter 1990 results reflected an unexpected loss and multi-million dollar shareholder lawsuits were filed) and the stock price was correspondingly depressed, some employees looked for quick fixes that that would solve our problems and make the stock market sit up and take notice of what we believed was a good company. Bill Esrey, though, repeatedly admonished that quick fixes were not the solution, that our objectives should be to stay focused, to work hard, to improve the company in little ways every day, and to build on a strong foundation for a great company. He emphasized that a prolonged record of strong and improving financial results quarter over quarter was what would impress Wall Street over time. He was right, and it taught me not to pay attention to daily or even monthly stock price fluctuations.

Indeed, I became quite skeptical of some stock traders. It outright amazes me that so much money seems to change hands in the stock market daily (if not hourly) based on the slightest, often incomplete (if not inaccurate) information about the issuer. Some people buy and sell based on the advice of some analysts or investment advisors who have horribly inadequate credentials. I can recall specific instances when panic caused some telecom stocks to markedly rise or fall because of an interpretation of an event or expectation by an analyst that was completely baseless. The good news is that the stock market does seem to correctly assimilate information and value good investments over longer periods of time. So my advice to the people who may be lured by the recent phenomenon of "day trading" is to recognize that your odds are no better (and maybe worse) than if you fritter away your money on the gambling boats.

Centel Merger

The acquisition of Central Telephone Company ("Centel") in 1992 was a little out of the ordinary for the new Sprint, and somewhat of an interesting story.

In 1990, Bill Esrey had established a secret task force (called the Strategic Review Challenge Team) to review acquisition opportunities. I was part of that team (headed by Ted Schell, and included Ben Watson, Don Goldman, Dave Scott and others) that met offsite for at least a couple of days each week from the end of April through November, to analyze a wide variety of possible strategies to achieve the company's ultimate goals. We looked at Centel (among dozens of other possibilities), but concluded essentially that its stock was overpriced (due to an expected acquisition premium).

Centel, seeking to maximize shareholder value, subsequently put itself on the trading block. It established a records room in Chicago where potential bidders could perform due diligence, and offered all or parts of the company at auction on a date certain. Sprint chose not to participate, and the date came and went with no announced winners. Instead, Centel called, explained that no one made a satisfactory offer, and urged Sprint to consider a merger. Esrey entered into talks that led to a deal at an exchange ratio below Centel's existing stock trading price (once again demonstrating Esrey's negotiating prowess).

The stock price reflected value to Sprint, but Centel's shareholders (especially the arbitraguers who were banking on big profits) were outraged, and some subsequently sued. One particular prominent investment advisor engaged in tactics (that seemed extortionate to me) designed to get Sprint to increase its offer, but Esrey kept his focus on Sprint stockholders (not speculators) and resisted.

Shortly after the deal was announced, Ben Watson (who Bill Esrey had named to head the merger transition team) called a meeting of the officers of both companies in St. Louis (halfway between the headquarters cities of Chicago and Kansas City) on June 1-2, 1992, to get to know one another and begin the planning process. Ben oversaw the entire process in what I thought at the time was somewhat of an overly administrative manner; but I subsequently had to admit that his efforts produced one of the smoothest and efficient merger transitions that I had experienced at Sprint. In particular, the preparation enabled Sprint to achieve more and faster savings from that merger than had been predicted.

The regulatory approvals of the Centel merger were also somewhat interesting. The DOJ once again (like they did in the US Telephone acquisition and the formation of US Sprint) raised the question of whether Sprint should be subject to an AT&T-like Consent Decree because Centel would add measurably to the local market power of the United Telephone System. They focused specifically on Las Vegas (Centel's largest serving area), but we were eventually able to persuade them that the market impact was of little consequence, since at the time all of the long distance traffic from that community roughly equaled the traffic from a single building — the Sears Tower — in Chicago. Las Vegas has subsequently become one of the fastest growing cities in the United States.

In any event, once we convinced the DOJ staff to approve the deal, we faced a timing problem. Bill Clinton had been elected President (but not yet inaugurated), and the Republican appointees at the DOJ were preparing to vacate. We needed the sign-off of the Assistant Attorney General-Antitrust, and he was literally packing boxes in his office as we asked for his approval. He was reluctant to bind his successor, and the situation was further confused by the nanny-controversy over Clinton's first choice (Zoe Baird) for U.S. Attorney General. We held our breath, got the approval and closed the deal.

Once the merger was complete, a number of Centel folks bailed out. The most noteworthy was Jack Frazee, the CEO who had pledged to stay, but who clearly was not having fun being number two. Al Kurtze stayed and went on to make an important contribution at STV and Sprint PCS. We also consolidated the Centel office in Washington, D.C., but lost everyone in Government Affairs except Grover Bynum (about whom I initially had reservations, but who proved to be an energetic employee and good friend). But even he left in 1999. The result is that Centel is a mere memory.

EDS

Not all of Sprint's merger opportunities did work out, though, which arguably was for the best. A prime example was the negotiations with EDS (given the code name by Sprint's Strategic Planning Department of Project Talking Horses). As Sprint's business with large corporate customers grew, we began to better understand the important role played by system integrators in purchase decisions. Sprint came to believe that an alliance between a successful system integrator — like EDS –- and its long distance (especially data) operations could be a powerful force in the marketplace. MCI apparently agreed, since they subsequently acquired SHL Systemhouse (but later sold it to EDS).

The talks with EDS soon led to merger proposals, but they eventually broke down over rather significant disagreements about the future prospects of each company's stock price. (A year or so later, it turned out that Sprint's forecasts had been more realistic.) The parties pledged to continue talking, but some bad feelings between the two prevented any real progress. Subsequently, Sprint satisfied the need for in-house system integration by acquiring Paranet in Houston, Texas (although the potential of that deal has yet to be fully realized). And EDS, now headed by Dick Brown (who formerly worked for Sprint, as well as Ameritech, H&R Block, and Cable & Wireless), has entered into a marketing alliance with MCI/WorldCom.

One of the lessons I learned from the EDS talks involved the due diligence process of examining each other's business risks. EDS had retained a Washington, D.C. law firm to look into Sprint. They peppered me from October 1993 through February 1994 with constant voluminous requests for seemingly meaningless documents — like copies of the hundreds of Sprint's radio licenses with the FCC — supposedly to establish whether Sprint had the appropriate government operating authority. I kept trying to explain to them that there were other documents (like internal reports to management about pending regulatory threats) that would give them greater insight into Sprint's business risks. But they seem determined to produce quantity (perhaps to increase the size of their client's bill) rather than quality information. I've always been a little skeptical of the motives of some outside law firms, and this experience did nothing to change that. I don't think my experience contributed to the breakdown of the talks with EDS, but it certainly seemed symptomatic of that ill-fated deal.

NFL

Sprint's two-year sponsorship of the National Football League (NFL) was very visible and, therefore, successful. Before that, Sprint was inundated with requests to sponsor a wide variety of professional sporting events, and found some — like some PGA and LPGA golf tournaments, soccer games, college basketball, the U.S. Ski Team, etc. — to be helpful in reaching potential customers. But the costs and results were somewhat scattered, and the company needed a more disciplined and dramatic approach to sports sponsorships. A very bright and courageous Sprint marketing executive, Tim Kelly, proposed negotiations with the NFL and produced a very beneficial contract.

One of the legendary stories to come out of those negotiations concerns the NFL coaches' headsets. Reportedly, when the basic deal for stadium advertisements, promotions, tickets and all the rest were about to conclude, the NFL attorneys mentioned that Telex's contract to put their logo on their headsets was about to expire. Sprint agreed, for about only a million dollars a season, to assume that contract and place just the Sprint logo (the split white diamond) on the earpiece of each NFL coach (except the Dallas Cowboys, who at that time preferred to negotiate their own deals) during every game. Given the proclivity of the TV networks to take head shots of NFL coaches on the sidelines during the games, the deal gave repeated and prolonged national network exposure to Sprint.

Ironically, that exposure ultimately led to the demise of Sprint's contract with the NFL. The NFL came to realize the tremendous benefit to Sprint of having the logo displayed repeatedly and calculated that it would have cost Sprint about $80 million to buy a comparable amount of TV advertising. Thus, the NFL sought to increase Sprint's cost of the sponsorship by approximately that amount when it came up for renewal. Sprint objected since, while exposure of the logo was clearly beneficial, it did not equate to advertising (because the Sprint name, 800 number and other messages were not displayed), and charges based thereon couldn't be justified. The NFL thought it had leverage, but Bill Esrey has never been known to make bad deals, and the contract was not renewed for the 1999 season.

I understood, but was saddened by the demise of the NFL contract. There had been several Government Affairs opportunities when we were able to leverage Sprint's relationship with the NFL to our advantage. And, I must admit, I was consistently impressed with the professional, well-planned and first-class way the NFL always conducted events. But business is business.

RadioShack

In 1997, Sprint embarked upon a retail marketing alliance with Tandy Corp., which inaugurated the rather new concept of a store-within-a-store. Specifically, new retail displays of Sprint products and services — including Sprint PCS phones and service, long distance services, calling cards, telephone equipment, etc. — were placed on dedicated displays in RadioShack stores around the country. This was not only a new and invigorating venture for RadioShack, but was a tremendous opportunity for Sprint to rapidly and comprehensively expand its retail presence throughout the United States. The numbers are amazing. There are 6,000 RadioShack stores nationwide, with 25,000 employees selling to the one million people who visit those stores everyday. Moreover, those RadioShack stores are located so that 94% of the U.S. population is within a five-minute drive of at least one.

To kick off this new alliance, Sprint representatives addressed the meetings of RadioShack sales representatives to prepare for the fourth quarter (called by RadioShack, because of the holiday selling season, as the "Golden Quarter") held around the country. I was assigned to attend the meeting in Los Angeles, California, on September 21, 1997, and was enormously impressed by what I experienced. My childhood impression of RadioShack was that it was a place in the mall to buy electronic parts, batteries and portable radios in stuffed animals. But I learned at the Golden Quarter meeting that they are well trained, highly skilled, clearly focused, motivated and energetic people who take great pride in developing lasting relationships with customers and beating sales objectives. Their enthusiasm was infectious, and I became convinced that Sprint had made a brilliant move by aligning with RadioShack.

Rolling Stones

Another brilliant promotion by Sprint was its sponsorship of the Rolling Stones' Bridges to Babylon tour in 1997. That was the first time that a long distance company had lent its name and resources to a series of concerts by a rock and roll group, especially one as notorious as the Rolling Stones. And the logo adopted for ads — the drawing of Mick Jagger's tongue with Sprint's pin stuck through it — was even more daring. But the magic touch of Tim Kelly (who subsequently and unfortunately left Sprint) once again turned it into another successful Sprint promotion.

The plan was to offer tickets to the concerts in each city, in advance of them going on sale to the public, to people who called and subscribed to Sprint's long distance service. The reaction was tremendous. Every concert in every city sold out, and Sprint gained thousands of new customers (and subsequent tracking showed that most of them stayed as customers long after the concerts were over). That success became a model for future promotions in many industries.

One of the Rolling Stones tour stops was in the new Jack Kent Cooke stadium in Washington, D.C., on October 23, 1997. Sprint's Government Affairs office in Washington arranged to sell (we could not give them away, due to ethics rules) hundreds of tickets to Members of Congress, their staffs, White House personnel, other government officials and the press. The Sprint special events folks worked hard and did a marvelous job making sure everyone had a great time. They also arranged for a number of VIPs to meet with the Stones backstage for a few minutes before the concert began. It was very chilly that evening, but the music was great. My favorite memory was spending some time during the concert with Senate Minority Leader Tom Daschle's wife, Linda (who is a lawyer in the Washington office of Howard Baker's law firm, lived for awhile in Kansas City when she worked for the FAA, and is a former Miss Kansas), who is a genuinely delightful young lady.

Compaq

In 1998, I had the honor of being asked to join the Telecommunications Advisory Board of Compaq Corporation. I had worked with Sprint's sales team (capably led by Denee Hawthorne) to try to sell more service to Compaq, and had always been impressed by the way Compaq had deftly adjusted to changes in the PC market over time to become hugely successful. Their idea to form this Advisory Board to gain a better understanding of telecommunications technology and direction, as well as the needs and plans of their customers and suppliers, was entirely consistent with what I learned was Compaq's unceasing determination to stay ahead of the curve.

The Board meetings were well organized, substantive (although often over my head in technicalities) and provided a fascinating insight into the future of both the telecommunications and computer industries. I was particularly impressed by the young officers of Compaq who met and worked regularly with the Board. They are very bright, energetic and dedicated people.

They had just completed their merger with Tandem Computers, and during my time there entered into the merger agreement with Digital Equipment Corp. It was apparent that they were struggling a little with the challenges presented by those mergers (not having had the same experiences with mergers as Sprint), but I believed they had the capabilities to learn and grow from the process. Eckhard Pfeiffer was revered as their CEO, and I'm sure his subsequent departure was demoralizing, although I suspect that hiring his replacement from in-house appeased many employees. But I have no doubt that the people of Compaq will emerge from the current difficulties to become an even bigger and better company.

CHAPTER FIVE

The Telecom Act

FEW REMEMBER IT, but I contend that the Congressional activity that eventually led to the Telecommunications Act of 1996 (the Telecom Act) began 20 years earlier. In 1975, AT&T and the integrated Bell System promoted legislation to essentially reverse the federal court decisions a year earlier (in the MCI cases) by declaring that the provision of telephone service in this country was a natural monopoly and that competition should not be permitted. With her enormous political power, Ma Bell was able to persuade a few hundred Members of Congress to co-sponsor the proposed legislation, which became known as the "Bell Bill." Yet, despite the initial support, the bill never went to a vote of the Commerce Committee, much less the full U.S. House of Representatives.

Why? Because people soon realized that such legislation would not benefit consumers, but only the old AT&T. That realization started the debate over whether and, if so, how competition should be introduced into the telecommunications marketplace. The issue was debated to some extent in almost every subsequent session of Congress. Things cooled a little when Rep. Lionel VanDeerlin — who had championed reform legislation — was defeated for re-election, but got serious in 1984 when the D.C. Circuit Court entered the Consent Decree divesting the BOCs from AT&T.

Many of the early legislative proposals (including the Danforth bill, the Brooks bill, the Dole bill, etc.) basically reflected the provisions of the Decree, providing that local telephone markets should be open to competition upon various terms, and that the line of business restrictions imposed upon the BOCs (especially the long distance ban) would be lifted when certain conditions were satisfied.

The debates were prolific and prolonged, which made for good theater during Congressional hearings. I testified on behalf of Sprint before at least a half dozen different Committee and Subcommittee hearings over the years on subjects like the AT&T Divestiture, Universal Service, access charges, international issues and the specifics of certain legislative proposals. While it was an honor to formally appear before Congress, I have to admit that all those hearings seemed to have little meaningful impact. The real work was almost always behind the scenes.

The effort to pass telecommunications legislation seemed to reach a crescendo when the Republicans took control of Congress following the 1994 elections. I remember, in particular, a meeting on December 20, 1994 (after the elections, but before the new Congress had convened) when Bill Esrey, Jim Lewin and I met with Senator Larry Pressler (R-SD). Pressler was designated to assume the Chairmanship of the Senate Commerce Committee (from Fritz Hollings) and was preparing to tackle the telecommunications issues. It was during the holidays, so we all had to fly in to Washington. We met at National Airport and drove to Pressler's office on Capitol Hill. It was an odd meeting. Pressler had a peculiar reputation (there's a legendary story — I don't know if it's true — about him trying to leave the Committee room one day during a hearing, but mistakenly walking into a closet, staying there for a few minutes, then exiting and waiving behind him as though he'd just met with someone in there). He lived up to that reputation that day. He had his staff show us an outline of what he wanted the legislation to contain; it was very troubling to us, but he didn't seem to care. Despite (or maybe because of) his shepherding of the telecommunications legislation in the Senate, he was not re-elected in November 1996.

Lobbying Coalitions

The seemingly constant and comprehensive federal legislative proposals gave rise to large, expensive and aggressive lobbying coalitions on both sides of the issues. The BOC coalition (that wanted the long distance ban lifted immediately) reportedly spent up to $20 million in some years to gain the support of legislators. The long distance coalition (that wanted bona fide and widespread local competition before the BOCs were allowed into long distance) was not as cohesive or well-funded. It was a real challenge for AT&T, MCI, Sprint and others to put aside their competitive dispositions in order to cooperate, but their coalition was effective (because, I believe, the concept of competition, rather than monopoly, was right and therefore easier to sell to Congress).

The long distance coalition was initially headed by a retired AT&T executive, but eventually employed Howard Baker (former Senate Majority Leader from Tennessee, and President Reagan's Chief of Staff). Howard (who later married Senator Nancy Kassebaum from Kansas) was an honorable leader, but unfortunately presided over the coalition during the time of the postcard scandal (we hired a grass-roots organization to generate postcards favoring our position to Members of Congress, but they used an old subscriber list and some of the signatures were from people who had died years earlier).

In any event, all of the lobbying activity (at least in my view), actually prolonged the process. Congress understood this was a battle of corporate titans who could afford substantial campaign contributions, which flowed freely whenever legislation was introduced and/or hearings were held (and slowed when there was little legislative activity). In some years, the political contributions from the telecommunications industry exceeded those of all other industries, and I became concerned that Congress would never pass a bill for fear of being cut off from that mother's milk.

It was pathetic, and I believe to this day that legislation finally passed primarily because Congress grew weary of being bludgeoned by both sides. I've heard it said that Congress often passes the right legislation, but usually for the wrong reasons. That was certainly the case here. There's another old axiom (by Will Rogers, I think) that the legislation is like sausage; you may like the final product, but you don't want to watch it being made. Believe it.

Synar Initiative

There was a point, in March 1994, when the debate over telecommunications legislation became particularly heated. The BOCs wanted provisions that allowed them into the competitive long distance market at precisely the same time that they opened their local telephone markets (a concept they called "simultaneity"). The long distance competitors, though, believed that local competitors actually had to be providing service as proof that those markets were in fact open, so they wanted the BOCs to lose some local market share before the long distance ban could be lifted.

In an effort to break the stalemate, Rep. Mike Synar (D-OK), a respected and thoughtful member of the House Telecommunications Subcommittee, stepped forward to try to broker a compromise. Mike generally supported the long distance position, so Rep. Rick Boucher (D-VA), who generally supported the BOC position, was recruited to give the effort balance. I knew Rick from my days at the UTS-Southeast Group. Rick is from Abington, Virginia (which is served by the United Inter-Mountain Telephone Company), and before his days in Congress was quite active on behalf of consumer groups in our rate cases. One of Rick's law partners (who was married to Howard Baker's sister) interestingly enough was a member of the Board of Directors of United Inter-Mountain Telephone Company. In any event, I always found Rick to be very skeptical (if not suspicious) of our position on the issues, although I never really understood why.

Mike asked both the BOC and long distance coalitions to name an individual who could represent their positions in negotiations; the long distance group named me. At the time I thought it was an honor, but dealing with the fractious group turned out to be less than fun. I met repeatedly with Mike and his capable staff for many late hours in his Congressional office. We drafted and re-drafted compromise provisions and sent them over to Boucher's office for review by the BOCs. The reply always came back reflecting virtually no movement away from simultaneous local and long distance market entry. Even though I felt we made meaningful compromises each time a draft was exchanged (and the other side did not), the process disintegrated when Boucher went public with some nasty (and I thought unfair) allegations about our willingness to cooperate. It was an unfortunate ending to what was, at least initially, a promising effort.

The exposure to Mike Synar caused me to become a big fan. He was reasonable, responsible, politically astute, knowledgeable of the difficult issues, determined to try to do what was best for the country and genuinely personable. I thought he had the potential to someday (if the Democrats maintained their majority) become Speaker of the House. Unfortunately, he was later defeated for re-election and, sadly, died (at a tragically young age) of a brain tumor. He was a good man, and his friends miss him a great deal.

The Act

The '96 Act is a massive piece of legislation, which covers a variety of subjects. It does not replace the 1934 Communications Act (except for a few select parts), but mostly supplements it. It is arranged in seven parts:

Title I	Telecommunications Services
Title II	Broadcast Services
Title III	Cable Services
Title IV	Regulatory Reform
Title V	Obscenity and Violence
Title VI	Effect on Other Laws
Title VII	Miscellaneous Provisions

Title I is the most important to Sprint. It declares that all incumbent local telephone companies in this country should make local interconnection arrangements available to competitors, and the BOCs are given the incentive to do so by being allowed — once they had done certain things to facilitate interconnection by competitors (according to a so-called 14-point "competitive checklist") and there was a legitimate competitor actually serving their customers — to enter the competitive long distance market in their regions. The logic was (and had been since the Consent Decree) that once there were competitive alternatives to the BOCs, they would no longer have the means or opportunity to harm competitors and, thus, could enter the competitive market on a fair and non-discriminatory basis.

Title I also addresses the conditions upon which the BOCs can manufacture telecommunications equipment, can engage in electronic publishing (both of which were also prohibited by the Decree), and can conduct alarm monitoring and private payphone services. Title II deals with ownership and licensing of broadcast spectrum (which has no real applicability to Sprint).

Title III deals with reform of Cable TV regulation, and is not a very pretty example of government in action. In 1984, Congress perceived a number of abuses by Cable TV operators and passed a law requiring regulation of monthly rates by the FCC. The Cable TV industry hated regulation and, even though they had obvious monopolies in each of their markets, fought the law. In 1992, Congress caved in to the pressure and passed another law abolishing Cable TV rate regulation. Thereafter, not surprisingly, Cable TV rates rose, service quality declined and customer complaints flooded into Congress. So, in the 1996 Act, Congress split the baby; that is, it authorized the re-regulation of Cable TV rates by the FCC, but only for three years (until March 1999). We have now come full circle, twice, and it's hard to say that anyone — except the Cable

TV lobbyists — have benefited.

Title III also contains provisions to encourage telephone companies to provide competitive Cable TV services, via reduced regulation (including preemption of franchising authorities), investments, and open video systems. Unfortunately, none of these incentives have worked, at least to date. Title IV permits the FCC to forbear from regulation where it's not necessary and can promote competition. These are great platitudes, but asking a regulatory agency to do less regulation on its own incentive is not proving to be especially workable or satisfactory.

Title V, although not directly applicable to Sprint, has a couple interesting provisions. It contains the so-called "V-Chip" provisions, which will enable parents to block their children from watching violent programming. It's now being implemented, but I continue to wonder how long it will take technology-oriented kids to circumvent the system. Title V also contained the provisions prohibiting obscene TV programming, which were subsequently struck down by the courts as unconstitutionally vague.

Titles VI and VII are legalistic, but contain some relevant provisions. For instance, they abolish the old AT&T and GTE Consent Decrees, allow the BOCs to provide long distance service from their wireless (cellular) telephones, and establish extensive rules for privacy of customer information by all telephone companies.

Vail Accord

It's a little known story, but Sprint played an important role in developing the requirement in the Telecom Act that competitors must actually exist in local markets before the BOCs can be allowed to provide in-region long distance service. In early April 1995, we hosted a conference of selected Congressional Members and staff at Vail, Colorado (at that time, Congressional lobbying rules permitted such outings). During the business sessions, we talked a lot about the need for legislation to open local telephone markets to genuine competition. The mood in Congress, though, was not favorable to objective measurements (e.g., market share tests) for determining how much competition was enough.

One evening, Bill and Julie Esrey graciously hosted a dinner for all attendees in their magnificent new home overlooking Vail. Rep. Jack Fields (R-TX), then Chairman of the House Telecom Subcommittee, and Rep. Mike Oxley (R-OH), the next ranking Republican Member, asked to meet an hour or so early to discuss this difficult issue. Fields and Esrey basically worked out the concept of requiring the existence of actual competitors (regardless of market share).

I discussed the details with Fields on a flight to Houston the next morning, and Fields incorporated it in the legislation when the Subcommittee met to mark up the bill for final approval. Sprint never took public credit for this accomplishment, but that may prove to be one of the most important parts of the law.

Essential Elements

Given Sprint's involvement with the formation of some of the critical provisions of the Telecommunications Act, we believed it was important to articulate specifically what we believed was required for local telephone companies to open their markets to competition. Sprint believed, because of its interests in both local telephone and competitive markets, that it could act as an "honest broker" in the process of defining such requirements. So we developed a comprehensive list — which we labeled the "Essential Elements of Local Competition" — of what needed to be done for genuine local telephone competition to take hold.

Subsequently, we submitted those Essential Elements to the FCC in its rule-making pursuant to Section 251 of the Telecommunications Act to adopt specific local telephone competition guidelines, and we were quite pleased when the final rules (adopted August 8, 1996) closely reflected our input. Those rules, following prolonged appeals, are now in effect and hold the promise of finally bringing genuine competition to local telephone markets. Assuming that promise will soon be realized, Sprint should be proud of its important contribution.

USTA Speech

Congress believed that the BOCs wanted so much to provide competitive long distance service (presumably packaged with their local offerings) that they would willingly give up their local monopolies. On reflection, though, the BOCs chose not to fully open their local markets, but tried to "game" the process by allowing only enough competition to gain approval to provide in-region long distance service (so that they could preserve their virtual local monopoly stranglehold). My view is that approach was not only unlawful, but bad business for the BOCs.

I was not shy in expressing my opinion in a number of public forums. To confront the issue head-on, I was asked to address a meeting of the Board of Directors of the United States Telephone Association in April, 1997. USTA (the successor to USITA) is comprised of local telephone companies and is mostly dominated by the BOCs (who joined after their divestiture from AT&T). The full text of my remarks follows:

"Thank you for the opportunity to speak with you about some of the important and difficult issues facing our industry. Although we are often (it seems) on the opposite side of many issues, Sprint believes that keeping open the lines of communication is proper, polite and productive. Sprint and USTA have a long history of association and cooperation. Although we are not now a member, we still value our relationship and respect the organization and companies that comprise USTA. It is because of that respect that I accepted your kind invitation to be here today, and intend to talk frankly with you. I don't think you want hollow praise or platitudes from me, and that's not what you're going to hear.

"I've known some of you since my early days in Sprint's local telephone operations. My perspective has been shaped over the years by working in both Sprint's local and long distance divisions. At Sprint, we believe that we take a balanced view of most issues, necessitated by our diversity. I have some strong personal views, though, and I will try to distinguish them where they may differ from Sprint policy.

"Let me start by emphasizing that Sprint's objective is to achieve a competitive telecommunications market. We are an active proponent of competition because we believe it's the best way to bring the highest quality, greatest value and advanced technology to the marketplace, because it's best for consumers, and because (frankly) we think we can successfully compete.

"Sprint, as most of you know, used to be a company called United Telecom, which prior to 1980 was a nice, profitable, relatively small telephone company serving primarily rural and suburban areas in over a dozen states. Then we made the strategic decision to enter the competitive long distance market, which was facilitated by the AT&T Divestiture (especially the creation of LATAs) in 1982. By the time the Divestiture was implemented in 1984, we'd acquired a reseller (U.S. Telephone) to help add customers and generate revenue while we were building the nation's first (and still only) all-digital fiber optic network. In 1986, we joint ventured with GTE Sprint to form US Sprint; and in 1989, we agreed to buy-out GTE and re-named *the company simply Sprint.*

"The point of the story is that competition works, and Sprint is living proof. Over the past 15 years, the growth of Sprint has been (I believe) one of the most important success stories in American business annals. Besides being on the leading edge of technology and product innovation, we've doubled the number of employees, we've tripled the company's asset value, and we've increased annual revenues seven-fold.

"Our success, though, didn't come easy. We were a monopoly which thought our basic telecom skills were all we needed. We were wrong. It was difficult for us to learn how to compete. We used to talk about being customer-focused, without having a clue as to what that meant. We know now. In fact, last year — in case you haven't heard — Sprint won the J.D. Power Award for the best customer service in the long distance industry; which was the first time in the 120 years since Alexander Graham Bell invented the telephone that someone other than AT&T was rated first. I tell you all of this, not to blow our own horn, but to help you understand our preference for competition, and to try to convince you that competition is an opportunity to be seized, not despised.

"I think one of the basic reasons why the LEC [Local Exchange Carrier — industry terminology for local telephone companies] *industry has apparently not embraced local competition during this past year is different understandings of the import of the '96 Telecom Act. I, like some of you, was in the trenches during the years of Congressional debates, and think I came away with a pretty good understanding of what was intended. I'd like to share my view with you, and hopefully you won't fundamentally disagree.*

"Congress was frustrated with the seemingly never-ending decade of litigation before Judge Greene that resulted from the ambiguity in the language contained in the AT&T Consent Decree (or Modified Final Judgement). Thus they were determined not to repeat the problems of the past and chose not to include in the new law a test like whether the Bell Companies could harm competition. Instead, Congress declared that local telephone competition was the new national policy and directed the Bell Companies to implement the 14-point 'competitive checklist' designed to open local markets.

"But since we (as a country) have never introduced local competition before, Congress put in another test to ensure that the 'checklist' would work. That is the requirement that the Bell Companies prove the existence in every state where they propose to

provide in-region long distance services, the presence of a facilities-based local competitor providing service to both residential and business customers.

"*The theory behind this requirement was that if the Bell Companies implemented the 'checklist' everywhere in a state, and real local competition actually developed somewhere in that state, then it should be able to develop anywhere in that state; and that was enough to assure that the Bell Company's monopoly power was sufficiently dissipated to allow it to enter other competitive markets. Some of the Bell Companies have not, though, completely accepted this interpretation of the law and (in my opinion) are trying to bend the rules to achieve entry into the in-region long distance market before local competition is real. But the local competition has to be real — not de minimus in amount or a sham. That's the only was the law will work.*

"*Unfortunately, some of the Bell Companies are asserting that the facilities-based competitor requirement is only a technicality and can be satisfied by simply signing interconnection agreements with small players who hold very little promise of viability, or by issuing public statements about agreements with larger players that haven't been implemented yet. Now, I'm not saying that the Bell Companies or other LECs are not entitled to their interpretation of the new law, and they certainly have every right to test the law and assert their position in court, especially to protect their assets, earnings opportunities and shareholder investments, as they see fit.*

"*My point is that we, as an industry, need to achieve real local competition and not try to game the process. I appreciate that it's hard to give up a monopoly. On that subject, as I said before, Sprint can speak from experience. In that regard, even though about a third of Sprint's business is incumbent local telephone operations, we are not particularly worried about exposing it to competition. We will certainly lose some share as competitors enter our local markets, but we believe any losses can and will be more than offset by the improvements we're making in the business to be more efficient, effective and attractive to customers, and by the new opportunities in other and adjoining markets which we fully intend to exploit.*

"*I do not believe, in other words, that competition is a zero-sum game. I believe that competition can, does and will stimulate the market and generate growth to everyone's benefit. Take AT&T for example; its smaller piece of the larger pie has enabled it to grow to a larger company today than before the advent of competition. Thus, strict adherence to the law, especially the implementation of real local competition, is critically important to both our and your future.*

"As you are all well aware, in order for the Bell Companies to obtain in-region long distance authority, they must do essentially three things: (1) prove to state and federal regulators that they've satisfied the 14-point 'competitive checklist,' (2) show the existence of a bona fide competitor providing local telephone service to residential and business customers predominantly over its own facilities, and (3) establish that their entry into the market is consistent with the public interest, including a competitive evaluation by the U.S. Department of Justice. Several Bell Companies already claim they satisfy all of these requirements, and we expect some of them to file with the FCC to enter the in-region long distance market within the next few weeks. I have to admit to you that I have mixed emotions about these proclamations.

"Some of the (smartest) Bell Companies have signed up to resell Sprint long distance service; we are pleased and proud to have them as customers and obviously wish them great success. Moreover, we've long made it a standard practice at Sprint not to criticize our customers. But we urge everyone — the state and federal regulators, and especially the Bell Companies — not to lose sight of the fundamental objective; that is, to achieve genuine local competition.

"Local competition is beneficial not only for the economic reasons that I mentioned earlier, but because it's the best and most effective means to prevent the monopolistic abuses that gave rise to the Divestiture 15 years ago. When the Bell Companies no longer have bottleneck control over access to local telephone customers, they will no longer have the means and opportunity to discriminate against long distance competitors.

"Competitors who feel abused or even threatened by the Bell Companies will have the ability, if local competition is real, to simply take their access business elsewhere, which provides a powerful incentive to behave and play fair. Bell Companies will then, just like all other competitors, succeed or fail based upon their own ingenuity, skills, hard work and attractiveness to customers.

"The message I'm trying to communicate here is that Bell Companies, anxious to enter the in-region long distance market, should not try to satisfy the entrance requirements with only a pretense of local competition. It is in everyone's interest that local competition be actual, demonstrable, sustainable and substantial.

"In that regard, let me share a personal fear with you. I believe

the Bell Companies' entry into the competitive long distance market is not going to be as much fun for them as they apparently think. Indeed, based on Sprint's experience, I believe it's going to be particularly harsh for those Bell Companies that aren't prepared to lose. Keep in mind that most other entrants into this market in the past two decades have experienced significant start-up loses, and there's no reason to believe the Bell Companies will be significantly different.

"*I should explain that my enthusiasm for long distance competition is the main reason for my frustration with local telephone companies that are fighting the change. I'm convinced that competition is the right outcome, and have little sympathy for those telephone companies engaging in tactics that are apparently designed to preserve their monopolies (and, therefore, an unfair advantage) for as long as possible. My personal belief is that these reluctant telephone companies are also doing themselves a great disservice. Local competition is now our national policy. It's right and it's going to happen everywhere throughout the United States. And, because of the WTO Basic Telecommunications Agreement reached in Geneva on February 15, competition will soon prevail around the world.*

"*Thus, the companies that are spending their resources trying to prevent or prolong local telephone competition are going to be ill-prepared when it happens. The winners in this contest are going to be the ones who start early and learn the skills needed to succeed in a competitive environment.*

"*So, faced with the impending local competition, the USTA Companies have (in my view) a big choice to make. Your choice is between turning your companies into competitive dynamos — by changing your culture, becoming truly customer focused, streamlining your operations, constantly seeking efficiencies, and becoming innovative, or by reacting badly to competitive inroads by using your monopoly market power to disparage competitors, gain an unfair advantage or otherwise harm competition.*

"*If you choose the latter, we will surely have — instead of competition — a level of litigation that our industry hasn't seen since before the AT&T Divestiture (which could very well result in another or series of divestitures). While I am personally not opposed to full-employment for regulatory lawyers, I do not believe such litigation serves the best interests of our industry or, especially, the consuming public.*

"*So, let's talk about some specific activities that I find particu-*

larly offensive. At the top of my list is USTA's 1997 Repositioning Campaign. The facts that (1) you've gotten together, (2) agreed to spend $12 to $20 million on collective advertising, and (3) chosen the theme 'Call Them On It,' indicate to me that you've (a) decided that long distance carriers (who are, incidentally, your largest customers) are the enemy to be publicly reviled, and (b) at least tacitly agreed not to compete against one another. I strongly believe that your actions have severe antitrust implications, and I can assure you that potential plaintiffs — including Sprint — are presently analyzing their legal rights and remedies.

"Please understand that I'm not saying that you shouldn't advertise. Advertising, particularly to build brand recognition, has become a necessary and expensive aspect of our business. What I'm trying to say is that your campaign gives the appearance of improper collusion, which makes competitors very nervous. And, the heated rhetoric in the press only aggravates the situation.

"In that regard, I'd like to share some of Sprint's early experiences with advertising. When we first entered the market, we thought that trying to denigrate our competitors was bold, bound to win-over customers and great fun. I still have copies of some of our early TV ads, and they are embarrassing. We learned pretty quickly that customers don't care about petty squabbles between big companies. What they want to know is what are you going to do for them. That's why (although AT&T and MCI at times don't seem to have learned this lesson) you don't see competitor-bashing in today's Sprint ads.

"A final bit of unsolicited advertising advice: Don't rely exclusively on your PR firm. Bozell Sawyer Miller Group are good, creative folks, but remember, they get paid whether the ads work, offend, or even land you in court. Exercise control over the message and content, and use the good judgment that's historically been the hallmark of our industry. My personal rule of thumb is that if I'd be ashamed or embarrassed for my family to know that I sponsored an ad, it shouldn't go on the air.

"Let me shift to other and somewhat related issues. Specifically, Access Reform and Universal Service. I must admit to you that I don't understand why we are arguing and why the arguments have grown so bitter. We all know that (1) access subsidizes local service rates, (2) the Telecom Act requires that those subsidies have to be (a) targeted, and (b) replaced by Universal Service funding and, therefore, (3) access rates must and will be reduced. Why, then, are we arguing over access reductions? Don't your own numbers on file *at the FCC show that access rates are significantly above costs? Why do you get so exorcised when MCI says access must be reduced by $14 billion? Why don't you agree, but point out that the shortfall must be made up by Universal Service funding so subscribers in high-cost areas can afford local service? Isn't the real issue the amount of Universal Service funding? Why don't we focus the debate on the real issue?*

"In that regard, your claims (in both your lobbying and advertising campaigns) about access cost decreases that long distance carriers allegedly do not pass along to consumers are disingenuous and, frankly, offensive. Long distance prices have decreased overall at greater rates than access charges in each and all of the past ten years, and you know it. I've seen some of your yield reports where you identify such reductions. If you don't want to discuss those numbers, look at publicly reported profits; your margins are more than double those of long distance carriers and are growing.

"Moreover, you've cleverly focused on only access rates and don't mention to the public that you've in reality raised other costs to long distance carriers — like payphone payments. The FCC is, as directed by the Telecom Act, privatizing your payphones and thereby generating a billion-dollar annual windfall for you (in the amount of $45 per phone per month for dial-around activity).

"You're supposed to remove payphone costs from access charges, which should be an offset, but it's not happening. Bell South just last week announced plans to put its 172,000 payphones in a separate unregulated subsidiary (which will make it the largest payphone operator in the U.S.) next month, and it has not reduced access charges at all.

"While we're on the subject of advertising claims, I have to give you credit for your long distance 'lock step' pricing argument. It's very clever. You've actually got some people thinking that all long distance prices have increased, and that price-following indicates a lack of competition, when the facts and economics are the opposite. Comparing and emulating prices is what aggressive, flexible and responsive competitors naturally do in a free market. Look at automobiles, airlines, groceries and other commodities. But you've hoodwinked some people into believing that competition doesn't really exist unless some competitors are charging prices that are markedly different for substitutable services.

"You've also cleverly picked an obscure tariff rate that less than one in four customers pay each month (and it's not the same cus-

tomers each month) to use as your proof that long distance carriers are greedy. You choose to ignore, for instance, Sprint's extremely popular Dime-A-Minute rate, which AT&T and MCI have followed — downward. You should be above these misleading tactics, and I hope we see an end to them soon. After all, I seriously doubt whether they're having an impact on the consuming public, who are well aware of the dramatic decreases they've experienced in long distance rates in recent years.

"Indeed, I'm hopeful for a couple of reasons that the situation is going to improve. I don't think anybody is enjoying the current situation. I've been in this industry over a quarter of a century, and I can testify that the people who provide telephone service — not the quick-buck artists who we all know have and will come and go, but the folks with commitment — are not only smart, creative and hardworking, but they're good and decent. We are people who understand and take seriously the public trust. We will do the right thing.

"And, as I've said repeatedly, I believe competition is the right thing; and as more of you open your markets and start to enjoy the benefits of competition, I'm sure you'll heartily embrace it. Certainly, some (both companies and individuals) will not be able to keep up with the change, and they'll retire. But the survivors will surely thrive.

"Thank you, again, for this opportunity. I genuinely hope that I haven't personally offended anyone. I certainly did not mean to. I hope, instead, that I've stimulated some thought, and that we'll have a lively question and answer session."

I received polite applause and a few questions when I finished delivering this speech (which was better than the hostile reception I expected) and left Dallas that day hopeful that I'd made an impact. I received a few congratulatory notes from some of the attendees afterwards, but otherwise I saw no real change in the BOCs' attitudes toward competition. I guess it's too big a problem, like trying to turnaround a battleship in a bathtub.

In any case, I've reproduced this speech in its entirety (not because I believe it's the best speech I ever gave, but) because I believe it best summarizes my basic beliefs about the requirements of the law, the forces at work in the industry today, and the approaches that are necessary to survive and succeed. The BOCs obviously didn't agree and, although they had supported the final legislation, commenced to litigate almost every aspect of it. They succeeded in blocking the FCC's regulations to implement the Act in the 8th Circuit Court, but were overturned by the Supreme Court. SBC even found a District Court Judge in Texas that declared Section 271 to be an unconstitutional "bill of attainder," but that was ultimately reversed as well.

While my frustration and criticism was directed primarily at the obfuscation and delaying tactics of the BOCs, the sad fact is that not everyone at Sprint agreed with me. There are some very bright people in the Local Telecom Division (the old United Telephone System) who understand what the future holds, but others have found it particularly hard to shed their monopoly ways and accept competition. They've ignored the Sprint experience and spent their energies trying to preserve the past. They can't resist much longer, though, and will soon learn that Neanderthals became extinct for a reason.

Why It Hasn't Worked

I don't mean to belabor many of the points that I made in the USTA speech, but I believe what's happened since the Telecommunications Act of 1996 became law is a national tragedy. Title I of the Act clearly articulated the national policy of local telephone competition and mandated local telephone companies (especially the BOCs) to open their market for interconnection by competitors. Instead of honoring and complying with this mandate, though, the BOCs almost immediately sought to diminish or defeat the mandate (and thereby preserve or prolong their monopolies) in any and every sympathetic court they could find. It took the better part of two years for these lawsuits to eventually fail, but that didn't stop the BOCs.

If they couldn't defeat the law in the courts, they decided to kill competition in the marketplace by fortifying their monopolies through mergers. In the first three years after the Telecommunications Act became law, there were over a dozen mergers (or proposed mergers) or joint ventures (not counting the MCI/WorldCom-Sprint deal), including:

SBC-PacTel	MCI-WorldCom
NYNEX-Bell Atlantic	SBC-Ameritech
SBC-SNET	AT&T-TCG
GTE-Bell Atlantic	AT&T-TCI
AT&T-BT	AT&T-MediaOne
Global Crossing-Frontier	Qwest-LCI
AirTouch-Vodafone	Qwest-US West

The U.S. Department of Justice must bear much of the blame for letting, in particular, the BOC mergers proceed without first requiring them to open their local telephone markets in compliance with the law. I am not alone in that view; Gene Kimmelman, of the Consumers Union, in an article in the *National Journal* said: "For dealing with one-sixth of the economy, the telecommunications market, [the DOJ] flunks a test of meaningful antitrust enforcement."

The DOJ first allowed the SBC-PacTel merger, apparently without realizing that there was more to come. The NYNEX-Bell Atlantic merger was next, and it was attacked from all sides as an obvious attempt to eliminate potential competition (especially in New York City). There was even written evidence of communications (e-mails) between the BOC employees about Bell Atlantic plans to invade the New York market, which were thwarted by the proposed merger. Yet, the Assistant Attorney General-Antitrust declared that it was too difficult to prove a "potential competition" case, and he was unwilling to challenge the parties unless he believed he could prevail in court.

I found it preposterous that the DOJ would decline to intervene in a merger with such enormous national economic consequences without even trying. The result was that the floodgates were open. As Mark Cooper, of the Consumer Federation of America, in the same *National Journal* article said: "After that deal was approved, [the BOCs] thought, 'Jeez, we can get away with anything.'" Greg Simon, former domestic policy advisor to Vice President Gore, observed, the BOCs "said 'Let us loose and we will compete with everybody.' They didn't say 'Let us loose and we are going to buy everybody.'" But, with the NYNEX-Bell Atlantic case as precedent, the DOJ was virtually foreclosed from challenging the subsequent SBC-Ameritech and GTE-Bell Atlantic mergers.

The BOCs have promised to compete once their mergers are approved, but that rings hollow. If they have genuine intentions to compete against one another, then why aren't they doing it now (and for the past three years)? The BOCs are clearly the best positioned companies in this country to compete against each other. They have the knowledge, experience, trained employees, financial resources, technical expertise and market knowledge to enter each other's territory and provide a competitive alternative, but they don't. The obvious conclusion, in my opinion, is that the BOC mergers are anti-competitive because they will eliminate the best potential competitors to themselves.

To explain their actions (or inactions), the BOCs assert that they need greater size to compete in global markets. But the fact that there are hundreds of small and successful competitors in the market disproves the contention that the BOCs have to be $50 billion in size before they can compete. This, as FCC Commissioner Susan Ness cleverly observed, is not Summo Wrestling.

The truth seems to be that the BOCs want the critical mass to be the masters of their own destinies, and they don't want a free and open competitive market where consumers have the ability to pick the winners and losers. Their scheme is so obviously anti-competitive (to me) that it's hard to understand why the government (after going through the agony of finally passing the Telecom Act) doesn't step up to the responsibility of enforcing the law.

In August 1998, Sprint formed a loose-knit team, dubbed SAGA (meant in an odd way to reflect the initials of some of the merging companies), to formally oppose some of the mergers, but Sprint's split-personality (with both local and long distance interests) got in the way of SAGA being very effective. Arguments against the anti-competitive aspects of the BOC mergers, for instance, often had to be severely tempered because Sprint's local telephone operations were found to covet many of the same objectives. It was very frustrating to be illogically restrained from doing what was obviously best (and inevitable) for the company. Even though SAGA spent a lot of time and money, the result was literally no significant impact on the process.

The DOJ lawyer who signed the original complaint against AT&T that led to the Divestiture was Phil Verveer. Phil subsequently moved from the DOJ to become Chief of the FCC's Common Carrier Bureau, and is now in private practice in Washington, D.C. (a partner at Willke, Farr & Gallagher). Sprint used Phil's firm to argue its case against the BOC mergers at the DOJ, and I believe he was as frustrated as I was with the outcome. Nevertheless, Phil is one of the most highly regarded, decent, honest and effective members of the D.C. legal community, and he's a good friend (and his wife is Hillary Clinton's Chief of Staff).

Soon we will have only four BOCs in this country (Bell Atlantic, SBC, Bell South and US West), and it's not unreasonable to expect one or more of them to merge into only two or even one mega-BOC. We will then, in my estimation, soon return to the days of wealthy monopolies and captured local telephone customers.

Another Gene Kimmelman quote: "Someday people will look back on this, scratching their heads, and say, 'How did we get so few companies, and how in the world do we get out of this mess of no one really wanting to compete?'" Brian Moir, of the International Communications Association, put it another way: "Never in our wildest imagination did we believe that the Antitrust Division would sit idly by as Humpty-Dumpty was put back together."

If the hard-fought Telecom Act is being so openly ignored, you may ask, then why doesn't Congress act to establish the rule of law? Good question. Unfortunately, though, some members of Congress seem to have willingly joined the BOC conspiracy. For instance, on July 1, 1999, a bill was introduced in the U.S. House of Representatives (by Rep. Billy Tauzin (R-LA), Chairman of the Telecommunications Subcommittee, and Rep. John Dingell (D-MI), senior minority member of the Commerce Committee) to substantially amend the Telecommunications Act of 1996, by letting the BOCs provide Internet service over long distance (which, in a digital environment, includes virtually all long distance services) while letting them maintain most of their local telephone monopolies for at least five years.

Specifically, the bill would require the BOCs to open their local markets to competition (not immediately, as required by the Telecom Act) but only in half of their territories within a year and a half, and the rest within three and a half years. This would give the BOCs plenty of time, it seems to me, to drive out any existing nascent and any future hope of local competition.

The good news is that there are still some honorable members of Congress who oppose this approach. Senator Ernest Hollings (D-SC) was a powerful influence in shaping the mandate of the Telecommunications Act of 1996 (and remembers clearly when the BOC lobbyists pledged to quickly open their markets) and views the BOCs' current intentions with great skepticism (observing that "None have complied [with the law] and in the past year none have even applied" to the FCC to properly enter the long distance market). The consumer can only hope that the principles of free and open competition will prevail over BOC bludgeoning of Congress.

The People

The story of the Congressional debates over telecommunications legislation is incomplete without a discussion of at least some of the people. I was engaged to some extent and traveled to Washington, D.C. regularly for 15 years (1984-99), and formed some lasting impressions and relationships. Most of them centered around Sprint's D.C. office. United Telecom first established a D.C. Office in the mid-1970s to monitor federal developments. We acquired the US Telephone D.C. office in 1984, and combined it with the GTE Sprint D.C. office in 1986, forming a separate US Sprint D.C. office. We combined the United Telecom and US Sprint D.C. offices in 1989. All these changes caused some turmoil and turnover, which limited our effectiveness. But in the 1990s we built an office that I believe had influence far beyond what the size of the company would have otherwise justified.

Leon Kestenbaum (who came from GTE Sprint's office and served in the FCC and other government offices before that) and his very capable staff represents Sprint's international and long distance operations before the FCC and federal Courts. For about two decades, he's been regarded as one of the most skilled and thorough communications lawyers in D.C. Jay Keithley (who I first hired to be General Counsel of the UTS-Indiana operations, and later headed United Telecom's D.C. Office) represents Sprint's local telephone operations at the FCC. He is a very learned, diligent and conscientious lawyer, and a genuinely nice person. These two guys have done remarkable jobs for Sprint for over a decade. The State Regulatory and Legislative function, which has a presence in the D.C. Office, was headed in Kansas City by Ellen D'Amato (who was General Counsel of Sprint's local telephone operations in Ohio, and switched jobs with Wayne Walston in 1990). Leon, Jay and Ellen (and Wayne) have been, as well as close associates, very special personal friends for a long time.

The Federal Legislative function in the D.C. Office, though, has experienced more turnover. Early on, the job was vacated due to some unfortunate and unpleasant personnel circumstances, and I had to find a replacement. In early 1991, I sought out Patricia Diaz Dennis, who had been an FCC Commissioner, was then in private practice, and was a special friend. She brought a lot of visibility and credibility to the office, and I enjoyed working with her. After a couple years, though, some personality conflicts arose and she opted to take an Assistant Secretary job in the U.S. Department of Commerce. The last I heard, she's an Assistant General Counsel at SBC in San Antonio, Texas.

I tried to run the Federal Legislative function in D.C. by myself for awhile, but quickly learned that I was over my head. The federal political process is unlike business. The way priorities are set, the way things get decided and done, and the way people interact with one another in D.C. are all considerably different than can be found almost anywhere else. So I went looking for a government insider. The D.C. office staff pushed me toward Jim Lewin, who worked for Rep. Jack Brooks (D-TX), the powerful Chairman of the House Government Operations Committee. I had tangled with Lewin during the debates that shaped the FTS-2000 procurement and some conflicts that subsequently arose. I had found him to be stern and somewhat calculating, but dedicated and deeply honest. The more I interviewed him, the more I liked him, and we hired him in November 1992. He's turned out to be not only a consummate political operative, but an excellent leader and motivator, and a close personal friend.

In December 1993, Jim introduced me to Sara H. (Sally) Smith, who was then a very effective Washington lobbyist for Pacific Telephone and had been a trusted staffer for years before that for Senator Thad Cochran (R-MS). Jim wanted to hire Sally as an Assistant Vice President. I had great faith in Jim's judgment, but was concerned about her recent advocacy of BOC issues. She alleviated all of my concerns, not only by the consistency of her beliefs (that local telephone competition should be both real and the precondition for BOC entry into the long distance market), but also by her genuine charm. She's a very special lady, and Sprint is very fortunate to have her as one of the leaders of the Government Affairs team.

At Jim's direction and urging, Sprint built some important and meaningful relationships with many influential members of Congress. As a result, I got to know, admire and genuinely respect a number of national figures. Senator Jack Danforth (R-MO) was a good friend to Sprint. I first met him at the University of Missouri School of Law, when he visited students during his 1968 campaign to become the first Republican state Attorney General since the Civil War. He won and put together an impressive office. His proteges included Kit Bond, John Ashcroft, Tom Coleman (former 6th District Missouri Congressman), Al Sikes (former Assistant Secretary of Commerce and FCC Chairman), Jack Craft (a prominent Kansas City Republican political operative) and U.S. Supreme Court Justice Clarence Thomas.

Senator Kit Bond (R-MO) is a genuinely good man. Jack Craft first introduced my wife and me to Kit when he ran for Missouri state Auditor 25 years ago, and we subsequently supported him in his races for Governor and Senator. He is not flashy, but works diligently to accomplish good things for the state and country. Moreover, family is very important to him and he's dedicated to his son, Sam. Kit both hosted a reception on Capitol Hill for me and entered a statement in the Congressional Record honoring me upon my departure from Sprint, for which I was deeply humbled and will be forever grateful.

Senator John Ashcroft (R-MO) is inspirational (and stands out, especially in these days when some in government demonstrably lack morals) and could very well be President someday. Senator Barry Goldwater (R-AZ) was a legend. I remember when my mother worked in his Presidential campaign. I was honored, when he served as Chairman of the Senate Antitrust Subcommittee, to testify before him on pending telecom legislative proposals. Senator John McCain (R-AZ) is a true War hero, but not always open-minded as a legislator. My impression was that he often impulsively seized positions on some issues and then refused to consider alternative logic. Senator Bob Kerrey (D-NE) is one of the bravest, committed and most sensitive men I have ever had the pleasure of knowing.

Rep. Tom Bliley (R-VA) is both a distinguished gentleman and a skillful legislator. As Chairman of the House Commerce Committee, he worked though some difficult obstacles (not the least of which was Speaker Newt Gingrich) to produce the Telecom Act of 1996. Rep. Billy Tauzin (R-LA) is a smart, calculating Cajun. He parlayed his conversion from Democrat to Republican into the Chairmanship of the House Telecom Subcommittee, and can be expected to assume even more leadership in future Congresses.

Rep. Jan Meyers (R-KS) represented Sprint's headquarters (the 3rd District of Kansas) very well for many years. When she retired, we hired the head of her Kansas City office, Mike Murray, who has turned out to be a very effective advocate for Sprint. Jan was succeeded by Rep. Vince Snowbarger (R-KS), who is a man of genuine conviction. He consistently placed his strong moral values ahead of politics (and, consequently, served only one term). Rep. Karen McCarthy (D-MO) works tirelessly to represent Kansas City (the 5th Congressional District in Missouri) and is a close personal friend.

I was also befriended by a number of very capable government staffers. There's a lot of criticism of government bureaucracy, but those folks truly make the government work. A good example is

Larry Irving. Larry was a legislative aide for Rep. Mickey Leland (D-TX) in the mid-1980s when I first met him. When Mickey died in a plane crash in Africa, Larry worked for awhile for Rep. Ed Markey (D-MA), then Chairman of the House Telecom Subcommittee. In the Clinton Administration, Larry was promoted to Assistant Secretary of Commerce to head the National Telecommunications and Information Administration (NTIA), where he did a remarkable job. He represents the best of what government can be, and I'll always treasure his friendship.

I had the opportunity (and sometimes challenge) to deal with the offices of virtually every FCC Commissioner the past three decades, under the chairmanships of Dean Burch, Dick Wiley, Charles Ferris, Mark Fowler, Dennis Patrick, Al Sikes, Reed Hundt and Bill Kennard. Most are very good, dedicated people, but they are often inundated with a plethora of issues and high-powered lobbyists. Thus, their staffs are critical to the process. Blair Levin, Chairman Hundt's Chief of Staff, was one of the best. He and Reed had a clear agenda, but Blair was always cordial and willing to listen and understand other views. I also need to express my admiration for a couple of current Commissioners: Michael Powell (son of General Colin Powell, who was a distinguished antitrust lawyer at the Department of Justice) and Harold Furchtgott-Roth (who was a staff economist for Rep. Tom Bliley on the House Commerce Committee during the Telecom Act debates, and is an articulate and stalwart conservative voice on the FCC).

Following the passage of the Telecommunications Act, in April 1996, Sprint hosted a meeting of a number of Congressional staffers in Orlando, Florida, to conduct a sort of post mortem on the legislation. It was a good exchange of what was done right and wrong in the process and what we needed to do to make the new law work. Attending, among others, was Mike Regan (who was counsel to Rep. Jack Fields (R-TX), Chairman of the House Telecom Subcommittee) and Carol Ann Bischoff, who was the telecommunications legislative aide to Senator Bob Kerrey (D-NE) (who had played a prominent role in assuring protection for rural telephone consumers). They met (I think) for the first time at our conference, and a romance blossomed. Today they're married and are wonderful friends. That may have been the best outcome of the entire legislative process.

I also had the pleasure to deal with many state and local government officials over the years. I first met Kansas Governor Bill

Graves when he was Secretary of State (when he married Linda Richey, who is both a special friend and a great First Lady of Kansas), and immediately liked him. He's an honest, decent and principled man, who could easily obtain higher office (but, due to his dedication to his family, will more likely spend his future raising his beautiful daughter).

I met the Reverend Emanuel Cleaver, two-term mayor of Kansas City, Missouri, when he was an active City Councilman. He's one of the most genuine, caring and concerned men I've ever met, and my life is better for having known him. He's not a professional politician and has chosen (at least so far) not to seek higher office, but to return to his church, which he could easily obtain.

There are many stories to tell about several others, but Senator Ernest Hollings (D-SC) is one of my favorites. Some of my fondest memories involve exploring different D.C. restaurants with Fritz and Peatsy Hollings and Sally Smith (whom the Hollings adore like a daughter). Hollings is a fascinating, opinionated and brilliant man, whose place in history is an important part of Americana.

But perhaps one of the most interesting political stories is how Bill Esrey came to support President Clinton for re-election in 1996. Esrey (like many Sprint executives) is a die-hard Republican, who supported Reagan and Bush in 1980 and '84, and Bush and Quayle in 1988 and '92. (Indeed, he developed a personal relationship with Quayle, Jack Kemp, Steve Forbes and others over the years). In 1994-95, though, the debate over telecommunications legislation began to heat up and people started taking sides. Senator Jack Danforth sponsored a compromise bill that contained many provisions acceptable to Sprint. We wanted to get Senator Bob Dole (R-KS), then Majority Leader, to sign on to the bill. Sprint was the largest private employer in Dole's state, and we believed he'd give our request due consideration.

We were, due to Dole's busy schedule, unable to formally meet with him during a visit to D.C. by Bill Esrey, except in the hallway for a few minutes outside a hearing room during deliberations on Clinton's contentious Health Care proposal. Dole was very agitated at Danforth that day (because Danforth had switched sides in the Health Care debate to try to facilitate a compromise) and insisted he would not support any legislative proposal with Danforth's name on it. Esrey pleaded with Dole that, regardless of personal emotions, the Danforth telecom bill was important to Sprint, but Dole stomped away. We were shocked and disheartened.

Following the encounter with Dole, we (Bill, Jim and I) had a meeting with Vice President Gore in the White House to talk about Sprint and our pending alliance with the French and Germans, as well as telecom legislation. We were pleasantly surprised when Gore and his staff treated us like visiting dignitaries. It was a very pleasant and substantive meeting, and I later came to appreciate that the White House, knowing it didn't have the support of big business in 1992, was consciously trying to build bridges to CEOs across the country. Bill remarked on the plane back to Kansas City that evening how incongruous it was that Gore (who we opposed in 1992) was so cordial and accommodating, while our local Senator was so abusive and uncooperative.

The Clinton Administration continued to support our position of telecommunications legislation and later, when Dole resigned from the Senate to run for President, the choice for Sprint was not difficult to make. Clinton subsequently asked Bill to host a gathering of prominent CEOs to endorse his re-election. Bill was not particularly comfortable, but he understood the importance of the event to Sprint's business and legislative objectives. (Indeed, the extent of Sprint's influence became evident when the President mentioned the company by name in the 1997 State of the Union speech). Clinton's personal transgressions in his second term were outrageous, offensive and embarrassing, and I suspect Bill personally regretted his association with the President. But I still contend it was the right thing for Sprint to have done at the time.

A little bit more about Al Gore. He was first elected to Congress in 1976, when I was in Tennessee, so I've followed his political career for some time. He served on the House Commerce Committee, which has jurisdiction over telecommunications, and I recall when I first visited his office on Capitol Hill.

I was met by Roy Neel (who was Gore's Chief of Staff in the House, Senate and White House, and subsequently became the outspoken head of USTA), who took me into Gore's office. Gore was at his desk working on a PC (it was unusual at that time for anyone other than secretaries to have PCs on their desks). I couldn't see what he was doing, but he made us wait for a few minutes while he finished. I came to believe that he was primarily trying to impress us with his technical prowess. It may be unfair, but I've subsequently viewed him with some reservation.

CHAPTER SIX

Wireless, International and ION

Sprint PCS

Personal Communications Systems (PCS) are the next generation of cellular telephone service. PCS is digital and lower power than analog cellular (which initially required car batteries), and thus able to provide more efficient and widespread mobile telephone service. The FCC, at the urging of Congress (for federal budget revenue purposes), decided in the early 1990s to auction radio spectrum for PCS to the highest qualified bidders. In July 1994, the FCC allocated 120 MHz (between 1850-1990 MHz) for broadband PCS, to be auctioned (by 1997, for over $20 billion) in six spectrum blocks:

Blocks	Channel Size	Markets	Licenses
A,B	30 MHz	51 MTAs	99 standard
			3 pioneer preferences
C	30 MHz	493 BTAs	493 entrepreneur
D,E,F	10 MHz	493 BTAs	986 standard
			493 entrepreneur

The market sizes were defined by Rand McNally's designations of Major Trading Areas (MTAs, about the size of states) and Basic Trading Areas (BTAs, about the size of large cities). The pioneer preferences were awarded before the bidding to companies that offered a new technological approach. The entrepreneur licenses were set aside for small businesses (the category initially included minority and women-owned businesses, but they were dropped after the Supreme Court's decision in the Adarand case).

Some of the entrepreneurs subsequently overbid and encountered great difficulty paying for, much less operating, the licenses. Eight of them — NextWave being the most notable — declared bankruptcy and generated a big legal battle over ownership of the spectrum. The issue was resolved by the Second Circuit Court of Appeals on November 25, 1999, when it overturned the U.S. Bankruptcy Court's ruling that had valued the spectrum at less than a quarter of what had been bid ($4.7 billion). The FCC is seeking to reclaim and re-auction the spectrum.

Sprint believed the future of wireless was in PCS and sought to become a major player. Esrey knew it would take deep pockets to be successful in the PCS auctions and (as he did during the construction of Sprint's nationwide fiber optic network) went looking for partners to share the burden. He wanted to do much more, though. In 1994, he negotiated a deal with three major cable TV systems — TCI, Cox and Comcast — to both pool their financial resources to bid in the PCS auctions and package local, long distance, wireless and entertainment services into a single offering for residential and business customers.

The negotiations were code-named Project Triple Play. The deal was concluded and announced in October 1994 and initially given the somewhat cumbersome name of the Sprint Telecommunications Venture (STV). We almost immediately started the process of obtaining needed regulatory approvals and trying to educate the government of the benefits of this business combination. We also started weekly conference calls of representatives of all the parties (which were almost too large and cumbersome to efficiently review our progress, but seemed necessary to keep everyone headed in the same direction), and gathered everyone together for a mass meeting in Kansas City in December 1994 (which didn't produce much substance, but promoted many working relationships).

Sprint soon learned, though, that upgrading cable facilities in order to provide local telephone access was going to be an enormously expensive proposition. Most cable plant had been constructed almost 20 years ago, and the cable operators had not done much in the way of maintenance. We learned, in that regard, that cable companies do not view themselves as being in the communications business, but in the entertainment business. Thus, they focus their energy and resources on content (programming) rather than on the delivery systems. Even those that had recently installed fiber plant used inferior quality facilities that would not readily support two-way telecommunications. The cost to upgrade this plant was almost as much as would be required to build a first-rate system from scratch.

Thus, the landline aspects of STV were quietly but rather quickly abandoned, and the focus turned to the wireless market. They formed a subsidiary for the purpose of bidding in the FCC's PCS auctions, and in March 1995 won 29 MTA licenses which, together with licenses held by venture affiliates, covered a population of 182 million, at a cost of $2.2 billion. STV, under the direction of Ron LeMay, became Sprint Spectrum and began constructing a nationwide system (which will cost, when complete, almost $10 billion). Sprint subsequently bid alone (spending another $2 billion) in the D & E Block auctions (the cable partners had lost their appetite for spending so much on radio licenses) and acquired BTA licenses to fill-out the nationwide footprint.

Andy Sukawaty was brought in to head the company, which was re-named Sprint PCS. As systems in various cities were turned up, sales exceeded forecasts. The service was crystal clear, easy and convenient to use, and priced moderately. And the business plan, to provide the only nationwide wireless service (using the same technology) in the market, was promising. The company grew by leaps and bounds, and in some respects was out of control (it reminded me, in many ways, of the wild and woolly days when US Sprint was a start-up). The losses were certainly reminiscent of the old days.

Sprint understood the need to incur losses while building a promising new business, but the cable partners were not having fun. The partners failed to approve a financial plan for the company for two consecutive years which, under the partnership agreement, triggered an opportunity for the partners to buy out one another. Instead of forcing a sale, though, Esrey commenced negotiations with the cable partners that eventually led to Sprint acquiring all of Sprint PCS by using Tracking Stock.

Tracking Stock was first used (I believe) when GM acquired EDS. GM owned all of EDS, but publicly issued stock that tracked the financial results of EDS, so that investors who were not particularly interested in the automobile business could follow (but not own) and potentially profit from the fortunes of EDS. In addition to creating a currency that enabled Sprint to buy out the cable partners, Sprint's investment banker (Dillon Read) advised that the new Tracking Stock would unlock value for investors in both Sprint's FON and PCS businesses. They were certainly right, because the price of both stocks rose quickly after issuance. Indeed, many stockholding employees became millionaires almost overnight.

Once Sprint PCS was wholly owned by Sprint in 1999, Esrey began the process of consolidation. Sprint was now almost a $20-billion company, but it was not taking full advantage of the possible synergies of having local, long distance, Internet, international and wireless operations under the same corporate umbrella. Esrey started a movement, called "One Sprint," to eliminate duplicate corporate overheads and combine network and sales operations. It's still a work in progress, and it's been very difficult for those at Sprint PCS who were infected with entrepreneurial spirit. Yet, as the company learned with US Sprint, it's natural evolution that maturing companies need to experience and must endure.

The Rise of Global One

In 1990, Sprint consolidated its data and network operations and turned the old Telenet organization into an international subsidiary. That company sought and obtained operating agreements with most major foreign countries, in order to sell Sprint's services around the world. They soon learned, though, that being a start-up in the global market was a tough road, especially once competitors started forming international alliances.

Sprint negotiated with British Telecom, but was not agreeable to BT's vision that it (and it alone) should own and operate a monolithic global network. Shortly after Sprint politely declined the deal, MCI entered its alliance with BT (which provided, among other things, that BT would own 20% of MCI, with a right of first refusal for the rest of its stock). It's rather well known that, when BT sought to acquire the rest of MCI in 1997, WorldCom upset the deal with a better offer. I'll always believe, though, that the FCC's denial of BT's desire to operate transatlantic circuits outside the international settlements process (which would have required BT to treat all long distance carriers the same as MCI, regardless of BT's ownership of MCI) had more to do with BT's lack of enthusiasm for MCI than WorldCom's hostile offer.

Sprint wanted to form an international alliance with France Telecom and Deutsche Telekom (who were closely bound by a European data alliance), but initially they were in talks with AT&T. So Sprint pursued the incumbent Italian telephone carrier (STET). FT and DT (like BT) wanted a substantial ownership interest in a

U.S. carrier, but AT&T was unwilling to satisfy that requirement, so FT and DT broke off talks with AT&T and called Sprint (who quickly put the talks with the Italians on hold). The negotiations were code-named Project Phoenix, and in 1994 the deal was made whereby FT and DT would each purchase a 10% of Sprint's common stock (a special class of stock was created for this purpose), and the three companies would contribute their international assets to a series of joint ventures that in the marketplace would be known as Global One.

It was a complicated transaction (like many that Bill Esrey had devised) that was difficult to explain to regulators and other government officials. We had to obtain approvals of the Department of Justice, the FCC, Treasury and Commerce (NTIA), all of whom were being lobbied by AT&T to reject the deal. (AT&T was obviously disingenuous, since they had sought to negotiate basically the same alliance with FT & DT.) It took a year and a half, but we finally obtained all needed approvals by the end of 1995.

The negotiations with the DOJ to reach a Consent Decree that would permit Global One to compete fairly in the worldwide marketplace were particularly intense and prolonged. We started to respond to the DOJ's request for documents and interrogatories in June 1994, and the process continued for a year. At that time, we also commenced weekly hour-long conference calls among the attorneys for Sprint, FT & DT, which proved to not only facilitate our efforts with the government but also built a strong bond between the parties.

In the heat of the summer of 1995, we reached the stage of face-to-face negotiations with the DOJ; which were conducted in King & Spalding's Washington, D.C. offices for days (and nights) on end. It was a grueling process, but I emerged with enormous respect for the professionalism, knowledge, concern and reasonableness of many of the people — like Steve Sunshine and Carl Wilner — at the DOJ. They worked hard to reach a deal that would both protect and promote global telecommunications competition. The Consent Decree was concluded and finally announced on July 13, 1995.

Hubbell

It was in late 1994 that I encountered Webster Hubbell. Since AT&T was pulling out all the stops to prevent government approval of Global One, Jim Lewin wanted to retain Hubbell to advise us on the content and effectiveness of our presentations to government audiences (but not the DOJ). I had lunch with Hubbell, and we agreed to retain his services for a limited period of time. Within a couple of months, though, his plea-bargain with the Independent Counsel was announced and we immediately terminated the arrangement (and Jim negotiated a settlement of the contract fee). The whole affair was brief, straightforward and harmless, which is more than I can say for the subsequent investigation of Sprint by the Independent Counsel's office.

The Independent Counsel apparently subpoenaed all of Hubbell's business records and discovered that Sprint was one of several companies that had retained his services during the period after he left the DOJ and before his plea-bargain. FBI agents (on loan to the Independent Counsel) interviewed us at length about our dealings with Hubbell. They were obviously suspicious about whether we'd been persuaded by individuals in the White House to provide financial aid to Hubbell, as part of a conspiracy to keep him from revealing information about the Clinton's involvement in Whitewater. We'd had no such contacts with the Clinton Administration, and no knowledge whatsoever of any such arrangements with Hubbell. Yet the Independent Counsel kept after us in the apparent hope that we would agree to provide testimony against Hubbell.

I recall one meeting when the FBI agents strongly but indirectly suggested that Sprint's image in the marketplace would suffer if we didn't agree to provide the assistance desired by the Independent Counsel. I subsequently checked with my superiors, and we respectfully declined to take a position that was inconsistent with the facts as I knew them. I believed that Hubbell, although he made some misstatements to us, provided us with useful advice (for which we paid him fairly) and, in particular, there was nothing improper about the relationship. Shortly after that message was communicated to the Independent Counsel, an article appeared in the Los Angeles Times newspaper (and quickly thereafter in other newspapers across the country) revealing that Sprint was one of Hubbell's clients. That story lingered for awhile, and clearly hurt our reputation.

The FBI shortly thereafter asked to meet with me again. I was infuriated and prepared to go into the meeting with a full head of steam. Jim Lewin counseled me, though, to stay under control and not exhibit any displeasure with the unwanted publicity. I took his advice, and the agents seemed perplexed that I was cordial and unconcerned about the recent developments. The matter soon died and the Independent Counsel seemed to forget about Sprint. The Independent Counsel's office was later accused of improperly leaking certain stories to the press. I could never prove it, but I was always suspicious of what happened in our case.

The Demise of Global One

The business plan for Global One was promising and had the potential to quickly position the venture to capture market share around the world. But Global One started life bloated. It had too much overhead, too many headquarters (one in Brussels, and one in D.C.), too many assets in some countries (and too few, or none, in others), and too many employees. And there were substantial cultural impediments to correcting these problems quickly. There were three or four employees — a Frenchman, a German, and one or two Americans — assigned to almost every job in headquarters. There was, initially, even two CEOs, and no one would insist upon layoffs for fear of offending the parent partner. After a year of more losses than were necessary, they did consolidate headquarters in Brussels and brought in a new CEO. He was a salesman, not an administrator, though, and the losses continued.

FT hosted a meeting of several executives of all three companies (called the Trilateral Conference) in Paris in early December 1996, to discuss solutions to the problems facing Global One. It was a very worthwhile meeting (and FT were most gracious hosts) and instilled a commitment (I believe) by most of the attendees from Sprint, FT and DT to pull together and succeed. The gathering facilitated subsequent communications among the parties, and there was real promise for the future; but the plans to make it an annual affair were thwarted by unexpected events, and expectations faded.

The international marketplace was becoming more competitive and by 1997, despite its problems, Global One had established a presence in 65 countries and was generating $1 billion in annual revenues. The following year, Sprint agreed to the appointment of Gary Forsee as CEO of Global One. Gary had all of the qualifications to make Global One work and become profitable, but the cultural problems (and thus the losses) persisted.

The Global One partnership agreement contains a provision (much like the STV agreement) that enables the partners to potentially buy out one another in the event they cannot agree upon a business plan for two consecutive years. That milestone was reached in early 1999, and Bill Esrey started the process of renegotiating the deal by letter to Michel Bon (FT's CEO) and Ron Sommer (DT's CEO). That letter was reported in the press as the first step in dissolving Global One, but that was not (in my opinion) Esrey's intent.

Esrey (I believe) wanted to take over Global One (much the same as he did US Sprint and STV years earlier), but had to be careful not to dissolve the 10-year standstill agreement (the press reported that restriction had expired after two years, but what had expired was FT and DT's right to block any sale by Sprint of a significant amount of assets) whereby FT and DT each agreed not to acquire more than 10% of Sprint's stock. The situation was further complicated by the deteriorating relationships between the partners.

FT and DT put up a united front throughout all of the negotiations that led to the Global One partnership. They seemed to believe that their strategies and ultimate destinies were inextricably linked (to solidify that link, they arranged to own 2% of the public stock of each other), and that they could accomplish more in the competitive global market together than apart. But that relationship began to sour when DT, without consulting with FT, stepped forward as a White Knight to help save Telecom Italia from Olivetti's hostile takeover bid. FT felt betrayed, and hard feelings soon developed, which were not alleviated when DT's offer to merge was rejected by Telecom Italia shareholders (by voting in favor of the Olivetti merger, instead).

The strained relationship between FT and DT negatively impacted the ongoing negotiations with Sprint over the future of Global One. The situation became both difficult and delicate for the management of Global One, which had to deal with conflicting directions from each of the three partners. Gary Forsee soon had had enough, and on June 30, 1999, he submitted his resignation. That was a terribly unfortunate development, in my opinion.

I first met Gary in 1988, when he was recruited away from AT&T to run Sprint's Government Services Division (GSD), which was created to fulfill Sprint's sales and service obligations under the FTS-2000 contract. Although I've never had much admiration for some AT&T alumni, I was genuinely impressed by Gary. He turned GSD from a rather rag-tag group (that had put together Sprint's bid for the FTS-2000 contract) into a professional, focused and successful sales and operational organization. He was subsequently promoted to President of Sprint's entire Long Distance Division in Kansas City, and instilled a financial, sales and operational discipline that produced record revenues and earnings.

Gary was not, in my view, treated fairly when Ron LeMay left for Waste Management and then returned to Sprint, but he was eventually compensated for his achievements by being named to head Global One in Brussels. That assignment in a foreign land turned out to be a hardship on Gary and his family; but he performed with his usual professionalism, focused Global One on a successful data strategy (creating the world's largest ATM-based network, with 1,400 access centers in 65 countries), and achieved annual global revenues of $1.1 billion. It was a big mistake to let Gary go; he's now a senior executive with BellSouth, and there is no doubt that company will benefit from his considerable expertise.

On January 26, 2000, after months of difficult negotiations, Sprint finally announced that it had reached a definitive agreement to sell all of its interest in Global One to Deutsche Telekom and France Telecom for $1.13 billion in cash and repayment of $276 million in debt. The agreement provides that DT and FT, who each own 10% of the common stock of Sprint, will vote their shares in favor of the Sprint-MCI/WorldCom merger (expected to take place at Sprint's annual stockholders meeting in April, 2000) and thereafter will relinquish their special rights as Class A shareholders and resign their seats on Sprint's Board of Directors. When the shareholder vote occurs, DT and FT will also be relieved of certain limitations on the transfer of their Sprint FON and PCS stock, and Sprint will relinquish its right of first offer (to acquire that stock) but retain certain rights to consult with DT and FT in connection with any sale of that stock. The deal is expected to take a few months to close, but DT and FT immediately assumed sole responsibility for the funding needs of Global One.

The deal does not mean that Sprint abandoned its international customers, though. The agreement provides for a two-year transition to assure continuity of service to Sprint's multinational customers who receive international service through Global One. Sprint was also released from certain Global One exclusivity and non-compete requirements, and simultaneously entered into an agreement with MCI/WorldCom that enables Sprint to sell MCI/WorldCom global services to its multinational customers (but is prohibited from offering competitive services to certain identified Global One customers for one year) going forward. Esrey assured customers "that Sprint will be able to deliver its complete line of international products, services and network support despite the change of ownership in Global One."

Later in the same day, France Telecom announced that it would acquire all of Sprint's and Deutsche Telekom's interests in Global One for $3.882 billion (or $4.346 billion, including debt), by paying DT $2.755 billion in cash and repaying $188.5 million in debt. These amounts mean that the total enterprise value of Global One at the time was $5.386 billion. DT quickly said that it was "pleased with the resolution with respect to the ownership of Global One," and that it would use the cash proceeds to further its international strategy through "acquisitions and majority shareholdings with strong partners."

The deal was viewed by analysts as beneficial for Sprint, primarily because it ended five years of losses that depressed the total company's earnings. Sprint had invested $718 million in Global One over time, and its share of the losses totaled about $650 million since 1995. Despite it's 35,000 business customers and 1998 revenues of $1.1 billion (and what I thought was great promise), Global One turned out not to be a good strategy or investment for Sprint.

Global One is a competitor to and inconsistent with MCI/WorldCom's international operations, so Sprint had little option but to sell its interests in Global One. MCI/WorldCom has undertaken to build its own international network facilities (much like they have in several U.S. cities) and not align (but compete against) foreign incumbent telephone companies. I used to think that was the highest cost and most risky international strategy; but the apparent failure of a number of international telecommunications alliances in recent years (including the now defunct BT-MCI Alliance, AT&T WorldPartners, Unisource, etc.) has changed my mind.

Sprint has also pursued other international opportunities, some in coordination with FT and/or DT and others alone. Sprint owns a 25% interest (the maximum direct foreign ownership allowed by current Canadian law) in Sprint Canada, to which it licenses its name, some technology and advertising. Sprint entered into a promising joint venture with Telefonos de Mexico (Telmex), which is partially owned by FT, to provide service to the Hispanic community in the southwest United States, but that deal sadly dissolved early in 1999. Sprint and FT bid on a competitive long distance license in Spain, and won such a license in Brazil. The future of those deals will surely be determined by MCI/WorldCom.

Internet and ION

It is becoming passe today to observe that the Internet is changing the way we do business and, to an extent, live. It's interesting to me how (and how fast) we got here. I remember an off-site meeting of Sprint executives conducted by Bill Esrey almost a decade ago when I first began to pay attention to the Internet.

We spent a very long day in a Kansas City hotel meeting room reviewing business results and strategic plans, and everyone was very tired by the time we gathered for dinner. The dinner speaker was a technologist whose topic was "The Internet; Who Cares?" He explained that government (DARPA) scientists had devised an alternative to burying telephone cables in six feet of concrete for protection against nuclear attack. The scheme was to build a geodesic network with multiple transmission paths so that, if any links were disrupted, constant communications could be achieved over various alternative routes. The speaker did not believe that this military system would ever have much commercial application. We joked about his presentation the next day, not because he was wrong, but because it was so boring.

What we didn't foresee at the time was the development of URLs (universal resource locators, or Internet addresses, like "http://www.sprint.com") and powerful search engines that would enable surfers to locate desired sites among the tons of information available worldwide. These tools enabled anyone with a PC and a modem to both access and have a presence on the Internet, and it seems virtually everyone has or wants to. It's a great new way to communicate, to research, to educate and to entertain. The future seems unlimited and I'm quite sure holds even more exciting and productive developments that we have yet to contemplate.

I'm also sure that Sprint's Integrated On-Demand Network (ION) will play an important role in the future of telecommunications. ION is a truly revolutionary development, and I'm convinced it's not yet widely recognized as such because it takes some historical context and explanation to fully understand. To start, Sprint's network (the nation's first and still only all-digital, fiber optic network) proved early on to be an excellent environment for high-speed data transmissions. Large business customers with the need for nationwide capacity and unfailing integrity for vast quantities of instant and constant data flocked to Sprint. Their demands gave rise to the need within Sprint to develop efficient, specialized and futuristic data applications. That group of scientists and engineers soon became a sort-of "skunk works" that generated many new concepts, including a whole new way of delivering telecommunications service.

Since the invention of the telephone, there's been a distinction between local and long distance service. Alexander Graham Bell's company first constructed lines to connect local customers, and only later build "Long Lines" to connect cities. As a result, regulation of telephone service developed a similar dichotomy; the Communications Act of 1934, for instance, provides for regulation of local service by the states, and of interstate service by the FCC. The local and long distance markets, thus, developed separately (with competition coming to the long distance market first) and the technology was engineered accordingly.

The nation's telephone system fundamentally operates on a "circuit switched" basis. That is, when you take a telephone "off hook," you are basically asking for permission to use the network, and if facilities are available, you are given a dial tone. You then designate the connection you'd like to make by dialing a number. If a circuit is available, the connection is made (if not, you receive a busy signal). The connection is the establishment of an electronic circuit, which remains dedicated to your call (and cannot be used for any other call) until you or the called party hangs up. Once a call is terminated, the facilities that comprised that circuit are then made available for other calls.

This method worked well for over 100 years, when most calls were of rather short duration, but the modern day requirements of large business customers (as well as some addicted Internet users) for data connections lasting many hours (if not days or weeks) began to unproductively tie up considerable quantities of circuits. While many in the industry looked for ways to restrict use and/or add more circuits, Sprint's engineers responded differently to the challenge. They started thinking "out of the box" and devised the integrated on-demand network. By August 1997, Sprint had assembled the marketing, network, regulatory, billing and customer service talent, under the direction of Kevin Brauer, to determine how and when to bring ION to market (the effort was code-named Fast Break).

ION essentially means that Sprint customers, instead of having to ask to use the network on a call-by-call basis, would be connected to the network (and their service would be "hot" and live) all the time. Such constant connections obviously require a great deal of network capacity, which Sprint accomplishes by employing dense wave division multiplexing. DWDM provides almost unlimited capacity by transmitting across a single fiber optic line dozens of different light waves, each distinguished and differentiated from one another by different colors.

This capacity, the constant connections and some remarkable proprietary network management software (that Sprint named "JCS2000" to honor one of the developers) will allow Sprint customers to be on the Internet virtually all of the time, to conduct continuing video-conferences (creating a "window" to remote offices, or even Granny's home), and to send or receive calls and/or faxes, all simultaneously if desired. Customers will be charged, instead of call-by-call, on the basis of the capacity. The initial price for ION customer service is $159.99 per month for unlimited Internet access (8 megabits per second downstream), up to four phone/fax lines (with custom calling features like Caller ID and call-waiting), and 2,200 minutes of "Distance-Free" calling (including local and domestic long distance), plus one-time installation and equipment charges. Since the incremental cost is low (after the up-front investment in the on-site network manager), over the long term customers (especially heavy users) should realize significant savings and productivity.

I believe that ION or its prodigy can and eventually will revolutionize not only the century-old method of delivering telephone service, but the technology also holds the potential to dramatically impact (and improve) at least parts of the economy. Just since the announcement of ION on June 2, 1998, Sprint has received expressions of interest from a wide variety of potential business customers. One of the most interesting (to me) is telemarketers. They run their businesses with large numbers of people working phone banks during, usually, four-hour shifts. Those employees (especially in rural areas) often have to drive long distances to sit in front of a computer terminal containing the information needed to make or receive calls.

Some telemarketers quickly realized that their employees and their business could be much more productive if they could avoid the commute (and the hassle of babysitters, etc.) and be able at home to receive and transmit over PCs the data they need, to make and receive calls and faxes to and from customers, and to additionally make or receive calls on their personal numbers, all at the same time (and at a cost that's probably less than the overhead of their telemarketing center). That prospect stimulates thoughts of even more applications for ION that could improve work-at-home and lifestyles immeasurably in the not-too-distant future.

The problem, however, is that Sprint (or, more particularly, Sprint's suppliers) apparently can't make ION work on a widespread basis today. The problems are, as I understand them, essentially two-fold. First is that the local high-speed digital access for customers to connect to Sprint's network are not readily available. The BOCs and other local telephone companies are promoting ISDN (integrated services digital networks) and/or DSL (digital subscriber lines), but both are expensive and neither have proven very satisfactory. The fact is, both are simply means of electronically enhancing the old twisted pair of copper wires to accommodate faster data speeds. It's like, in my view, strapping a V-8 engine to an ox cart. The only legitimate long-term solution is to eventually change out the copper with fiber optics, which will obviously take a lot of time and money.

In the meantime, people are also exploring other alternatives, like cable and wireless solutions. The Cable TV facilities that are in use today, however (as AT&T is learning) are old and inadequate, and it will take considerable funds to upgrade them as well. Some of the fixed-wireless proposals (like multi-channel, multi-point distribution service, or MMDS) hold some promise, but they are unproven in a widespread commercial environment. So the bottom-line is that there simply isn't any good way to get ION to a large number of customers across the U.S., at least for the time being.

Perhaps even more troubling are the problems Sprint appears to be having with its equipment suppliers. Sprint joined with equipment manufacturers, like Cisco and Tellabs, to build in mass quantities the network controllers and other gear needed to make ION work. The prototypes are impressive, but the process of producing the finished product in commercial quantities has been fraught with delays (which seemed to culminate in an announcement on November 24, 1999, that further development of JCS2000 would be abandoned).

The result is Sprint has been able to install working ION service for only a handful of customers. It announced that it will take orders beginning on November 15, 1999, for ION service only in Kansas City, Denver and Seattle. After all the initial fanfare about ION, Sprint has been rather stoic about the situation. A Sprint VP was quoted in the October 18, 1999 issue of *BusinessWeek* as saying that ION "is revolutionary, and when you do revolutionary things, there's not going to be overnight implementation."

An unnamed industry analyst, who was also quoted in the same magazine article, was less generous in his summation; he simply concluded that "ION is a joke." I strongly suspect that such harsh criticism played an important role in the decision to sell Sprint to MCI/WorldCom. The impact on the company's value in the stock market would surely have suffered if the failure of ION, especially after all of the fanfare, became widely known and accepted. The situation, in that regard, strangely reminds me of the story of RJR told in the book "Barbarians at the Gate." That story, if I remember correctly, is that RJR's CEO sought to buy up the company's stock (and thereby put the company in play, which resulted in his losing the company to KKR & Co.) before the news that the much-touted "smokeless' cigarette was a distasteful failure.

It's a shame because, as I said before, I think ION represents the future of telecommunications. I hope that MCI/WorldCom continues to pursue it, but there's little assurance that will happen. If they don't, though, someone else surely will. In that regard, I can't resist the urge to prognosticate some more.

There's little debate that the Internet is still in the nascent stages of development and that we've yet to see its great promise fulfilled. But I think the future impact of the Internet is more than just faster worldwide electronic communications. I think the Internet is bound to modify the mass media. Television, radio, newspapers and other publications today are geared toward mass audiences, and their content reflects the majority's interests. But the Internet is facilitating the delivery of much more personalized information to minority audience shares. I think that, as the technology evolves to permit access to the Internet by TVs (rather than PCs), the market for more select programming will blossom, if not predominate. In that new world, I believe ION (and its prodigy) becomes a household necessity.

CHAPTER SEVEN

Pending Industry Issues

MOST OF MY CAREER at Sprint was spent advocating the company's position on a variety of telecommunications issues before state and federal regulators and legislators. Because of the pervasiveness of the telephone (i.e., literally everyone has or has access to one), many of these issues have an impact on almost everyone in the United States. Yet I've always been somewhat surprised (or chagrined) that most of the issues are not widely understood. Perhaps it is because many of the issues are relatively complex. So, in an effort to help others understand them, I'd like to briefly describe some of what I think are the most important pending issues.

Local Interconnection

Congress required in Section 251 of the Telecommunications Act of 1996 that all incumbent local telephone companies should make interconnection to their local telephone networks available to new local competitors, so that the competitors can use all or parts of the existing networks to serve local customers. The law required the FCC to adopt regulations to implement such interconnection within six months of passage. The FCC just met that requirement and adopted comprehensive rules on August 8, 1996.

Those rules identified the separable parts of incumbent local networks (known as Unbundled Network Elements, or UNEs), and established methods for pricing of those parts based on costs (or default prices, if cost studies were not performed). The FCC's rules seemed favorable to competitors seeking to enter local telephone markets. But incumbent telephone companies (especially the BOCs) and some State PSCs were displeased and sought relief in federal court. Several appeals were filed, and they were consolidated in the Eighth Circuit Court of Appeals (in St. Louis), before a three-judge panel (headed by my old law school dean, Pasco Bowman).

The Court sympathized with the BOCs both initially (it stayed the effectiveness of the rules on October 15, 1996) and eventually (it overturned the rules on July 18, 1997). The Court also overturned two related FCC decisions, being (1) a rule allowing competitors to recombine UNEs (overturned on October 14, 1997), and (2) the FCC's use of the principles contained in the stayed rules when considering BOC applications (under Section 271 of the Telecommunications Act) to enter the in-region long distance market.

All of those decisions were combined in an appeal to the U.S. Supreme Court, which agreed to hear the case on January 25, 1998. Oral argument was held on October 13, 1998, and the Supreme Court (by a 5-to-3 vote) reversed the Eighth Circuit on January 25, 1999. So the case is now (as I write) back before the FCC to conform its rules with the Supreme Court's decision. There's been a lot of debate over how much, if any, of the FCC's rules should be changed (as a result of both the Court's decision and changed circumstances in the interim).

I personally believe that the FCC's original rules hold the best hope for real local telephone competition in this country. The fact that virtually no local competition has occurred during the three years that the rules were stayed by the courts is pretty convincing evidence, in my view, that they are needed to get the job done. Thus, I hope the FCC acts both courageously and quickly, and that the BOCs refrain from further appeals and finally comply with the law.

Universal Service

This may be the most complex case, but it is also (I believe) the most important (especially the dollar impact on the industry and consumers). To understand the issues, I think it helps to review a little history. Regulators have historically considered local telephone service to be a necessity and long distance service to be a luxury. Thus they've permitted (if not encouraged) telephone companies to price local service below cost (so that more people could afford a telephone) and make up the difference by pricing long distance above costs. Universal Service is the term coined (originally by AT&T) to describe the goal of reasonably priced local telephone service.

But the advent of competition in the long distance market had a dramatic impact upon the goal of Universal Service. Competition both drove down the price of long distance calls (toward the cost of providing the service) and stimulated long distance calling. The net effect was that local telephone companies, which charge long distance companies for access to local networks on a fixed, per-minute basis, made significant profits. Long distance companies argued the windfall should be reflected in lower access rates.

The debate caused Congress to substantially overhaul the Universal Service system in the Telecommunications Act of 1996. Congress specifically declared that all prices should be based on costs, and any Universal Service subsidies should be separately identified (rather than buried in long distance rates) and targeted (to high-cost areas and low-income users). The FCC was ordered to adopt rules to implement this new system and, on March 8, 1996, it established a Joint Board (comprised of state and federal regulators) to consider and propose such rules.

The Joint Board, though, has struggled with the issues, particularly the political aspects of Universal Service subsidies. States and local telephone companies who've lived on subsidies for decades don't easily give them up. The result has been a series of delays in (and appeals of) the needed decisions to implement the law. Although the FCC told the Joint Board on July 17, 1997 to propose new rules to be implemented on July 1, 1999, very little real progress has been made.

During this time, the FCC has nevertheless moved forward with the so-called E-Rate (or Gore Tax). Section 254(g) of the telecommunications Act permits the FCC to prescribe "preferential rates" for schools, libraries and rural health care providers. The FCC, at the urging of the Clinton Administration (especially Vice President Gore), adopted rules on May 7, 1997, that grant various discounts (depending upon need) on the price for telephone service to qualifying schools and libraries so that they may connect to the Internet. The amount of money needed to fund these E-Rate subsidies exceeds two billion dollars annually.

Congress contemplated that these funds would be redirected from existing subsidies (that would otherwise be eliminated), so no increase would result, but the FCC and Joint Board have been dilatory in the assignment to reform Universal Service. The result is that the FCC has had to increase the amounts of Universal Service subsidies paid by local and long distance telephones companies (although the local companies are allowed to pass their increased costs along to long distance carriers, so that long distance carriers bear most of the burden). Thus, while the Telecommunications Act was intended to promote competition and corresponding cost decreases, the FCC's handling (or mishandling) of Universal Service has produced just the opposite.

Access Reform

The Congressional mandate to permit interconnection and accomplish Universal Service reform required the FCC to reform access charges as well (the FCC referred to it as "the third leg of the stool"). Access charges are paid by long distance companies to local telephone companies for connections to customers. Since the per-minute rates presently support the old Universal Service, those rates were expected to be reduced (to costs) as the subsidies were eliminated. On May 7, 1997, the FCC adopted Total Element Long Run Incremental Costs (TELRIC) as the standard for determining the costs of access. But, since the FCC has failed to implement reductions in Universal Service, movement of access rates to costs has not, in any methodical way, begun.

Instead, the FCC has sought to drive down access rates by requiring local telephone companies to reduce them by the amount of projected annual productivity improvements. The FCC regulates the rates of major local telephone companies (especially the BOCs) by a system of Price Caps (rather than the old rate-of-return methodology). The BOCs can price their services anywhere below the Caps, and the FCC adjusts the Caps annually for inflation, productivity and other cost changes. On May 7, 1997, the FCC ordered the annual productivity factor increased to 6.5% (which would produce a reduction in access charges in a corresponding amount) for 1998. The problem is the BOCs thought that was too much and appealed the FCC's order; and the D.C. Circuit Court of Appeals reversed the FCC in May 1999. Thus any reductions in access charges are now in jeopardy.

At the same time, the FCC on May 7, 1997 also implemented a new kind of access charges to fund the E-Rate increases. They were flat, fixed rates charged by (1) local telephone companies on customer bills (called Subscriber Line Charges, or SLCs), and (2) long distance companies (called Primary Interexchange Carrier Charges, or PICCs). Sprint (and other long distance carriers) passed through those new charges on customer bills (about 80 cents per single residential line, $2.75 for multi-line business customers, and about 4.5% of the interstate and international total for Universal Service).

These new charges appeared to many customers as rate increases, which angered the FCC (because it had expected any increase to be offset by the productivity decreases). The fact is the FCC's failure to timely address Universal Service reform has produced the convoluted mess of current rates and special charges to the consternation of both carriers and customers. For that reason, a number of local and long distance carriers — including Sprint — joined together in early August 1999 to present the FCC with a compromise proposal to eliminate PICCs, establish a $650-million explicit Universal Service fund and eventually lower long distance rates, by doubling the SLCs (from $3.50 to $7 per month) on monthly local telephone bills.

I honestly believe that this proposal is the only economically sound way to resolve the current problems and correctly implement the law, but it does not have the support of the entire industry or consumer groups. The concern is that all local telephone consumers will see their monthly bills increase, while only those who use a significant amount of long distance (which is often higher income households) will see any offsetting rate reductions. While this opposition may seem compassionate, it ignores the fact that higher SLCs more properly recover costs from the cost causers (thereby doing away with uneconomic subsidies), which ultimately will permit fair local competition (which is bound to both improve technology and drive prices down). It will be interesting to see if the FCC can gather the courage to do the right thing.

BOC Long Distance

Section 271 of the Telecommunications Act says that in order for the Bell Companies to obtain in-region long distance authority, they must (1) prove to state and federal regulators that they've satisfied a 14-point "checklist" to allow interconnection by competitors, (2) show the existence of a bona fide competitor providing local telephone service to residential and business customers predominantly over its own facilities, and (3) establish that their entry into the market is consistent with the public interest, including a competitive evaluation by the U.S. Department of Justice.

Although no BOC has satisfied these requirements (evidenced by the fact that there's very little, if any, local competition), several of them sought permission from the FCC to enter the in-region long distance market in the first two years after the Telecom Act became law. A summary status of those applications is:

BOC	State	Date Filed	Status
Ameritech	Michigan	Jan 2, 1997	Withdrawn Feb 11
SBC	Oklahoma	Apr 11, 1997	Rejected June 26
Ameritech	Michigan	May 21, 1997	Rejected Aug 19
BellSouth	S.Carolina	Sep 30, 1997	Rejected Dec 24
BellSouth	Louisiana	Nov 6, 1997	Rejected Feb 4, 1998
BellSouth	Louisiana	July 9, 1998	Rejected Oct 13

This experience tells me that the BOCs were either trying to "game" the process by allowing a little competition and seeing whether the FCC will approve, or trying to wear down the FCC by repetitive applications, or both. Neither, in my opinion, will or should work. Indeed, the fact that the BOCs are able to manage the amount of competition that exists in their regions proves (at least to me) that the competition is not genuine. Customers, not monopolists, should control the amount of competition that exists in any free market.

Bell Atlantic filed the only application in 1999 with the FCC for permission to enter the long distance market (in New York state) under Section 271 of the Telecom Act. The FCC, given the amount of local competition in and around New York City (even though the Justice Department opined that there's still not enough local competition in the state), approved the application on December 22, 1999. The good news is that this decision will surely set a very high standard for the other BOCs to meet before they can be allowed to provide competitive long distance in their states.

Besides the unmeritorious applications to enter the long distance market, some of the BOCs have engaged in other questionable tactics in this area. The best (or worst, depending upon your perspective) example was SBC's attempt to have Section 271 declared an unconstitutional "bill of attainder." The attainder clause of the Constitution prohibits the legislature from imposing personal penalties, so that individual due process rights can be protected in the courts. The BOCs claimed the law keeping them out of the long distance market until local competition developed was an unconstitutional personalized penalty (even though in the 200-year history of the Constitution, the attainder clause had never been applied to corporations). SBC found a friendly judge in Wichita Falls, Texas, to rule in its favor on New Year's Eve, 1997, but the Fifth Circuit Court of Appeals (in New Orleans) reversed the decision on September 4, 1998 (which was upheld by the U.S. Supreme Court on January 19, 1999).

A couple of the BOCs — Ameritech and US West — tried another end-around Section 271 of the Telecommunications Act. They entered into long distance "marketing alliances" with Qwest, a start-up fiber optic carrier in Denver, to sell long distance service to their customers. The law simply says the BOCs cannot provide long distance (until they permit local competition and secure FCC approval) whether they do it themselves or by reselling someone else's long distance service. So the courts and the FCC quickly stayed the Qwest agreements, and the FCC ultimately found that they impermissibly violated Section 271 on September 28, 1998.

I have little doubt, though, that at least some BOCs will continue to try to find a back door into the in-region long distance market. They'll eventually wear out the regulators and courts, or elect enough friendly members of Congress to change the law, or develop new service schemes, or a combination thereof, just so they can keep competition out of their traditional monopoly business. The problem is they can't rewrite the laws of economics. Competition is bound to ultimately prevail, and, if it doesn't, my guess is that we'll see new divestiture litigation to make way for competition.

As an aside, I must say that Sprint seems to have been preoccupied with the potential of BOC entry into the long distance market for far too long. I started getting questions about when the BOCs would be allowed into long distance shortly after the AT&T Divestiture was announced in 1982. I was skeptical that Judge Greene would remove the line-of-business restrictions, but others disagreed. I recall, specifically, a memo written by Ron LeMay that predicted BOC entry within two to three years. A dozen years later, Ron made essentially the same prediction when the Telecommunications Act was passed. Having formerly worked for AT&T and Southwestern Bell, I suspect that Ron had much more respect for the capabilities and courage of the BOCs than I did. In any event, I used to jokingly retort that the BOCs wouldn't get into long distance until after I retired. Although I expected it to be a few more years, it turns out I was right.

WTO Telecom Treaty

The Telecommunications Act of 1996 proved to be not only good legislation for the United States, but a model for the world. While it was being enacted, the U.S. Trade Representative commenced negotiations with the member countries of the World Trade Organization ("WTO," the administrative organization that was created by the General Agreement on Trade and Tariffs, or GATT) to establish similar competitive principles for telecommunications markets around the globe.

Those negotiations produced the Basic Telecommunications Agreement (known as the WTO Telecom Treaty) in Geneva on February 15, 1996. It was subsequently ratified by the requisite number of countries and made effective on February 5, 1997 (at which time I was honored to represent Sprint at the White House news conference held by USTR Ambassador Charlene Barshevsky and FCC Chairman Reed Hundt).

The FCC then commenced proceedings to implement the U.S. commitments under the new treaty. The rules, adopted November 25, 1997, permit entry into domestic telecommunications markets (which had theretofore been limited by the 1934 Communications Act) if the rates charged by the foreign applicants to handle international traffic from U.S. carriers (so-called accounting rates) are at or below certain cost-based benchmarks. The initial benchmark rates are:

Foreign Country Classification	**Benchmark Rates**	**To Be Effective By:**
Upper Income	15 cents per minute	January 1, 1999
Upper/Middle	19 cents per minute	January 1, 2000
Lower/Middle	19 cents per minute	January 1, 2001
Lower Income	23 cents per minute	January 1, 2002*

This date may be extended until January 1, 2003 for countries with teledensity less than one (i.e. less than one telephone per 100 inhabitants).

Many foreigners did not like the FCC dictating their rates (especially since many of them charged rates well above costs in order to subsidize other functions, such as their postal services), and 40 countries appealed the rules. But the D.C. Circuit Court of Appeals upheld the FCC rules and they went into effect.

Thus, the regulatory environment for foreign carriers in the U.S. is now much more accommodating than Sprint faced when we sought approval of the alliance with France Telecom and Deutsche Telekom. And, probably more importantly, true competitive telecommunications markets around the world are now within sight.

Telmex/Sprint Joint Venture

On the international front, I also need to tell the story of Sprint's deal with Telefonos de Mexico ("Telmex"). When Mexico opened its telecommunications markets to competition, AT&T (via Alestra) and MCI (via Avantel) entered through affiliates. Sprint, though, chose to partner with the incumbent Mexican carrier (Telmex) to provide service to the Hispanic community on both sides of the U.S. border with Mexico. This approach required FCC approval (because of Telmex's entry via the joint venture with Sprint into U.S. markets), and the FCC was concerned with Telmex's accounting rate (which, at that time, was about 39.5 cents per minute). Telmex eventually agreed to satisfy the benchmark (19 cents by 2000), but that did not appease our competitors, AT&T and MCI, which continued to raise objections based on the treatment they received as competitors in Mexico. The result was it took over a year to secure the needed regulatory approvals to proceed with the joint venture.

In the meantime, business relations between Sprint and Telmex deteriorated. I must admit that I never fully understood why the parties eventually determined that the joint venture should be dissolved, because I always found the Mexicans to be earnest, engaging and easy to work with. I never met Carlos Slim Helo (the primary owner of Telmex), but worked a lot with Telmex's President, Jamie Chico Pardo. Jamie Chico and I often visited with regulators and legislators in Washington, D.C., and he was always a gentleman, was always well versed on the issues, and always was an effective spokesman for Telmex and Mexico.

I also had the pleasure of travelling to Mexico City in mid-October 1998, and the honor of meeting with Javier Lozano Alarcon, the President of the Comision Federal de Telecomunicaciones (Cofetel), the Mexican regulator, to talk about the development of competition. He's a very bright and dedicated young man, who clearly has a great political future ahead. Indeed, I got the distinct impression that there's an impressive generation of young Mexicans, many of whom have been educated in the U.S. and Europe, who are dedicated to improving the country's economy and raising Mexico out of the third world and into prominence in the international community. After meeting with Javier Lozano, I became convinced he will be a successful leader in that effort for years to come.

In any event, in July 1999, the FCC authorized Telmex (without Sprint) to operate as a competitor in the United States, and I strongly suspect that they will be successful.

Slamming

This issue is not the magnitude of the others (unless, of course, it happens to you), but it's a classic example (in my view) of government style over substance. Slamming is the slang coined to describe the situation when an unscrupulous long distance carrier converts a customer without his or her consent to its service. The unauthorized carrier hopes and expects that the customer will not notice the change (often because its charges appear on the local telephone company's bills) and pay its usually higher charges.

It is a problem that is caused by the fact that local telephone companies are required to treat all competitors on a non-discriminatory basis. That is, they must accept from all long distance companies orders to convert customers without questioning the validity of those orders. Crooked carriers quickly recognized the opportunity to slam customers and make a fast buck. When customers started complaining, the government got involved.

But the government, in its bureaucratic wisdom, decided it could cure the problem by imposing substantial penalties on slammers. The problem is that the government didn't bother to first understand what causes slamming, before fashioning a remedy, and the result is that the remedy doesn't work. Long distance carriers get changed without customers' consent for essentially two reasons: (1) by mistake (i.e., the data exchange between legitimate long distance carriers and local telephone companies gets inadvertently garbled), or (2) crooked carriers submit unauthorized orders. Penalties do nothing to correct either cause. In particular, crooked carriers don't pay fines; they simply skip town and reemerge elsewhere under a different name.

So what's the solution? I argued that the FCC should set up an independent agent between long distance carriers and local telephone companies to receive and verify the legitimacy of orders (and carriers) before they're processed. Independent agents already exist (to handle such things as telephone number administration), so this approach could be easily implemented. And I believe it would eliminate slamming (and probably most inadvertent mistakes as well) quickly and effectively. There's been some study of this proposal, and I hope something like it will soon be adopted.

CPNI

Telephone companies obtain a great deal of personal information about their customers — not just name, address and telephone number, but also how many calls and where you call each month, whether and how promptly you pay your bill, who you use for long distance service, what extra services you use, etc. This data, in telephony talk, is known as Customer Proprietary Network Information ("CPNI"). Traditionally telephone companies have been very circumspect in their use of CPNI. FCC rules required local telephone companies to use the data only for the purpose of providing service. But relatively recent concern over privacy rights gave rise to rules applicable to all carriers.

The Telecom Act specifically required the FCC to adopt CPNI rules applicable to both local and long distance carriers; and, on May 17, 1996, the FCC proposed that all carriers give confidential treatment to such data unless the customer consents to its use for marketing or other purposes. The FCC modified those rules slightly when they were adopted on February 26, 1997; they now require customer consent before a telephone carrier can use CPNI to market any service to that customer that's outside the current "family" of services being provided by that carrier. That is, a local telephone company can use a customer's CPNI to try to sell more or other local services to that customer, but cannot use the same CPNI to try to sell long distance services to that customer without his or her consent.

One of the most controversial aspects of these rules is whether a carrier can obtain consent from a customer to use his or her CPNI to market other services by means of a so-called "negative ballot." That is, can a carrier send a letter to a customer saying that it will use CPNI unless the customer notifies the carrier that he or she doesn't consent to such use. Besides the fact that such "negative ballots" are generally frowned upon in privacy circles, some carriers have used letters to customers that are so confusingly or arcanely worded that customers have little hope of understanding their rights. I personally received a notice in my monthly local telephone bill (from Southwestern Bell) that was difficult — even given my legal training and years of regulatory experience — to understand, much less to appropriately respond in order to protect my privacy. I predict, therefore, when consumers begin to realize how their usage data is being employed by telephone companies, that there will be an uproar and greater demand for more stringent FCC rules.

Detariffing

State and federal regulators have historically required public utilities to compile their rates and all other terms and conditions of the service they provide to consumers (known as tariffs) and make them publicly available in the commission's files. That process enabled regulators to closely monitor and control the service being provided to the consuming public (even though the public hardly ever checked those files). But, with the advent of competition, the FCC decided that the emerging competitive long distance carriers need not file federal tariffs (but could advise consumers of their rates in the same manner as other competitive companies in other industries). The courts, however, found that the FCC did not have the statutory authority to mandate detariffing.

Thus, Congress specifically authorized the FCC, in the Telecom Act of 1996, to detariff non-dominant (that is, those without market power) long distance carriers. The FCC, accordingly, proposed detariffing rules, but the federal District Court in Washington, D.C. stayed the decision. The FCC asked for a voluntary remand so it could change the rules in August 1997, to allow long distance companies to file tariffs covering the first 45 days of service provided to customers who select or change their long distance carrier through their local telephone companies. The FCC reconsidered the decision again in early 1999, requiring carriers to post their rates at their place of business. Argument before the court in the appeal of the FCC's rules is scheduled for January 2000.

Despite this legal wrangling, I believe that long distance carriers will eventually be completely detariffed, and will have to find another way to publish their rates. The Internet is an obvious alternative, but there are still many consumers in this country who don't have ready access to a connected PC, much less the World Wide Web. It probably means that in the future when new customers of long distance carriers receive their first bill, they will also get a rather bulky document with very fine print (that they'll likely never read) that sets forth all the terms and conditions of their new service.

Campaign Finance Reform

This country, in my view, is in desperate need of campaign finance reform. In the 1980s, I was used to getting calls from candidates and their campaigns asking for contributions in amounts from $500 to $1,000. Beginning in the 1990s, the requests started coming from professional fund-raisers and the requested amounts increased to $2,500 to $5,000. I don't know that the first Clinton campaign in 1992 was responsible for this escalation, but I question the coincidence. In any event, by the 1998 campaign, I was getting calls seeking corporate "soft" money in amounts of $250,000 to $500,000.

The situation has clearly gotten out of hand. The last Presidential campaign cost over $300 million. Think of the good that could be done with that money, instead of spending it on irritating, incessant and largely ineffective TV commercials. But what can be done? The McCain-Feingold bill would ban "soft" money (which are unregulated and unlimited contributions by individuals or corporations to the political parties or issues campaigns, not directly to the candidates), but the Republicans (who get more "soft" money than the Democrats) won't enact it.

I suspect McCain's "holier than thou" approach (he contends on this and other issues that he, and only he, knows what's best for the Congress and the Nation) also constitutes a substantial obstacle to passage of this legislation. I also question McCain's consistency, even though it was a centerpiece of his campaign for the Presidency in 2000, since my experience includes being at the receiving end of his volatile temper when we didn't perform to his expectations during his Senate re-election campaign in 1998.

My feeling is that we should eliminate all limits on contributions (especially those imposed after Watergate, since they've been antiquated by inflation), continue to allow Political Action Committees (PACs) so that individuals can maximize their impact by aggregating their contributions, and require all contributions from any source to be promptly and publicly reported (on the Internet, for instance, for everyone to see). That way the voting public can see for themselves who's supporting each candidate, and can judge whether the amount causes any concern about the possibility of undue influence. I trust the people to make good judgments once they're fully informed.

I came to this view largely as a result of a Kansas City, Missouri mayoral race. When Dick Berkley was seeking his unprecedented third term in 1987, Jim Heeter (a close personal friend) sought to challenge him. I helped Jim, but the campaign needed more funding. A local millionaire with an eccentric reputation offered to pour thousands into the campaign and, despite admonitions from some of his friends, Jim accepted. The amounts quickly caught the attention of the local press, and the millionaire's involvement was widely reported. The public was obviously worried about the possibility of undue influence, and Jim lost the election. I thought Jim would have made a marvelous mayor, but I learned to respect the power of informed voters. I believe that experience provides some useful insight into the cure for the federal problem.

Numbering

A few months after I retired from active employment with Sprint, Larry Strickling, Chief of the FCC's Common Carrier Bureau, called to ask me to consider replacing Alan Hasselwander (retired CEO of Rochester Tel, now called Frontier) as Chairman of the North American Numbering Council (NANC). NANC is a Federal Advisory Committee which provides advice and recommendations to the FCC on administration of the North American Numbering Plan (NANP) and national numbering issues, including local number portability (LNP). NANC is comprised of representatives from every sector of the telecommunications industry, Canada and Caribbean countries, the states and consumers. NANC meets monthly at the FCC's offices in Washington, D.C.

Although I've certainly been critical of the FCC in the past, I've known and had great respect for Larry Strickling for many years; and, therefore, felt an obligation to accept his invitation and try to make a contribution. Some of the folks at Sprint (who apparently still harbor petty grudges) tried to impose obstacles to the appointment, but Larry was very creative and found a way to get it done. Thus, I became Chairman of NANC at the September 28, 1999 meeting at the FCC's Headquarters in Washington, D.C. Although it's proving to be more work than I expected, I am enjoying the opportunity to meet with old friends (and make some new ones) and try to make a difference. Being (for the first time) on the government side of some challenging regulatory issues has also given me a new perspective on both the work of the FCC and the role of lobbyists.

The numbering issues facing this country are significant and pressing, but relatively unknown. The NANP was devised and first implemented by AT&T in the mid-1940s. It created the system of Area Codes which, for the first time, allowed direct long distance dialing (before then, you had to ask the operator to connect you to an operator in the distant city, who would complete your call).

Originally, in 1947, there were 86 area codes in the U.S. That number increased at a rate of about one new area code per year until 1994, when there were 134 area codes. In the mid-1990s, though, an explosion in the use of telephone numbers began, caused by the demand for second residential telephone lines (for facsimile machines, and to connect PCs to the Internet) and new wireless (cellular and PCS) services. In 1996, 22 new area codes were added; in 1997, 43 new area codes were added; and in 1998, 24 new area codes were added (bringing the total to 248 area codes). At this rate, if nothing changes, the available numbers in the NANP could be exhausted, according to some studies, as early as 2006.

The reason that existing area codes are being exhausted (and thus new ones have to be added) is not necessarily because we're running out of numbers, but primarily because of inefficient use (or more particularly, non-use) of existing numbers. In each area code, there are a little less than eight million possible telephone numbers (some — like 411, 911, 555-1212, etc. — are universally blocked for special purposes), but they are all not utilized in every area code. Telephone numbers are assigned, under the NANP, according to the Central Office Code (or NXX, the first three digits in each local telephone number) in blocks of ten thousand. However, not every Central Office (or computerized telephone switch) serves ten thousand customers. In some (especially rural) areas, a Central Office may be dedicated to serve only 1,000 customers, and even if every one of them used three numbers (for residential service, a fax and a mobile telephone), there would still be 7,000 unused numbers (that are not available to be used anywhere else in that area code). It's a waste, especially when we are running out of numbers in other places.

If nothing changes and we eventually run out of new area codes, one obvious solution could be to increase area codes to four digits (and thereby change everyone's telephone number from 10 to 11 digits). That kind of remedy has been employed in other countries (like England), to the great discontent of most users. There are at least a couple of better solutions, though, that can permit the FCC to extend the life of the NANP. One is to implement 10-digit dialing for all calls (which has already been done in several areas, particularly on the East and West Coasts). That frees the use of Central Office Codes in all area codes (which may have been blocked so seven-digit calls to one NXX would be routed to only one area code). It requires a change in dialing habits, and a lot of consumers resist change, but it's an easy and effective way to better utilize existing number resources.

Another solution is technology. Telephone companies are now, as required by the Telecom Act and FCC regulations, implementing Local Number Portability (or LNP, to permit customers who change their local telephone service provider to keep their existing telephone numbers, if they so desire). LNP requires, essentially, a series of data bases, which look up and connect calls to the service provider of the called customer's choice. An important side benefit of this technology is that it will permit the portability of whole blocks of unused numbers for use in places where existing numbers are being exhausted. In fact, the FCC has already ordered landline telephone companies to implement LNP in 2000, and wireless companies to implement LNP in 2002. If they stay on that schedule, it should provide considerable relief to the current pressures on the NANP.

However, implementing LNP for wireless companies on time will be a major challenge for a couple reasons. Wireless companies, for the most part, designed their systems to keep track of calls (for completion and billing purposes) according to the customer's identification number (known as the Mobile ID), rather than their telephone number (which is one of the reasons why directories of mobile telephone numbers are not easily compiled or readily available). Thus, in order to implement LNP, wireless companies will have to make major (and very expensive) systems changes (to convert to Mobile Directory Numbers). And, this financial burden comes at a time when wireless (especially PCS) companies are spending billions to build out their networks to achieve more and better call coverage. Since wireless companies are one of the causes of the faster consumption of telephone numbers, the fact that they are not in a good position to implement LNP (in order to provide some relief to the number crunch) is a real conundrum for them.

The good news is that NANC seems, at least in my view, to be well positioned to understand and evaluate the issues and to make sound recommendations to the FCC to solve the problems and thereby extend the life of the NANP by, according to some estimates, as many as 50 to 80 more years. The next couple of years, as we seek to implement such relief, should prove to be very interesting.

CHAPTER EIGHT

The Merger

THERE'S BEEN serious speculation at least since the 1996 Telecom Act that Sprint would be the target of one or more takeover attempts. Even Sprint has publicly acknowledged that there's been an acquisition premium in the price of its stock for the past few years. But according to documents filed with the government, it was Sprint that initiated the process that led to the merger deal with MCI/WorldCom. The Board of Directors of Sprint voted at their meeting (held in Paris, France) in June 1999, to authorize the officers of the company to approach potential suitors, including BellSouth Corp., Deutsche Telekom AG and MCI/WorldCom.

The Negotiations

Bill Esrey called Bernie Ebbers in July, and the talks quickly became serious. Both companies conducted "due diligence" of one another (that is, they researched and examined one another to fully comprehend all of the legal and financial consequences of a merger) for the next few months. By September, transactional lawyers for both companies were meeting regularly (and often late into the evenings) in New York City to write the extensive documents that reflected the precise terms of the agreements reached by the principals. It was (and often is) an exhaustive and exhausting process, and usually very profitable for the outside counsel (who bill by the hour) and the investment advisors (who take a percentage of the deal). In any event, the effort intensified toward a successful conclusion as news started to leak out about what was happening.

The intensity was heightened by some last minute maneuverings. According to Ebbers, agreement had been reached on a price (by a telephone call to Esrey on horseback in Colorado, using his

Motorola Iridium telephone), but within a few days BellSouth bested MCI/WorldCom's initial offer. Esrey met with BellSouth's CEO in New York City and declined the offer, saying he had to leave to get to another important meeting (presumably with Ebbers, at which MCI/WorldCom increased its offer). Sprint accepted Ebber's improved offer, and the deal was done.

Deutsche Telekom, although in and around the negotiations at all times, apparently never made an offer. Interestingly, DT's CEO, Ron Sommer, is a member of Sprint's Board and voted to accept the MCI/WorldCom offer, but FT's CEO, Michel Bon, did not. That was probably more a reflection of the split between DT and FT, though, than an indication of FT's opposition to the deal. In any event, I believe that DT will continue to be a factor. After all, DT wants to be a global player, and therefore needs a significant presence in the U.S. market, and Sprint is the most logical candidate.

DT's position as a Sprint insider could facilitate a competing offer (especially if MCI/WorldCom faces possible divestiture of desirable assets — like its Internet company, UUNet — in order to secure regulatory approval to acquire Sprint). DT has been embarrassed and therefore temporarily paralyzed by its rather public and unpleasant break (after long time, strategic and comfortable relations) with FT. But, given that the future is at stake, DT can be expected to recover and assert itself within the next year.

FT, on the other hand, is still encumbered by majority government ownership. Thus, it cannot be reasonably expected to act deftly enough to impact the ultimate ownership of Sprint. FT has, though, wound up with the consolation prize; that is, FT will acquire all of Global One. That outcome intensifies, in my view, the challenge facing DT if it truly wants to become a major player in the global telecommunications market. Ron Sommer, has said that he will pursue an international strategy through acquisitions and majority investments (some, presumably, in strong U.S. carriers). I, frankly, don't see how DT can resist going after ownership of Sprint or (perhaps), after the merger, the larger WorldCom.

The Deal

Regardless, on October 5, 1999, it was publicly announced that the Boards of Directors of both Sprint and MCI/WorldCom had approved a definitive merger agreement. The new company, to be called WorldCom, will generate pro forma 1999 revenues of more than $50 billion, will have a market enterprise value of approximately $290 billion, and will have operations in more than 65 countries. The companies expect the merger will be consummated in the second half of 2000, following approvals by their stockholders, the FCC, the Justice Department, certain state PSCs and foreign antitrust authorities.

There had been speculation for some time that MCI/WorldCom was interested in Sprint because it desperately needed wireless capabilities. In the merger announcement, Bernie Ebbers, MCI/WorldCom's CEO, said, "The merger with Sprint is particularly timely as wireless communications emerges as a critical component of full service offerings. Increasingly, wireless will be used for Internet access and data services, two areas in which both companies excel. Gaining an all-digital nationwide footprint with common technology and spectrum that delivers next generation capabilities is of paramount importance." The new company will have more than four million PCS subscribers and 1.7 million paging and advanced messaging customers.

The price paid by MCI/WorldCom represents an approximate $23-billion premium for Sprint and a $5.5-billion premium for PCS. The companies estimate that annual cash operating cost savings of $2 billion are achievable in 2001 (the first full year of operations), increasing to $3 billion annually by 2004, from better utilization of their combined networks and other operational savings. Based on these figures, MCI/WorldCom is paying a multiple of 24 times taxed and discounted synergies (which is twice the 10-15 times normally considered reasonable in such mergers). Yet the merger announcement said that the transaction is expected to be essentially non-dilutive to WorldCom's earnings per share before goodwill amortization. Thus significant cost cuts can be expected.

The total value of the merger is approximately $129 billion (apportioned at about $69 billion for Sprint, $46 billion for PCS, and $14 billion in debt and preferred stock). At the time of the announcement, it was the largest merger in American corporate history (the next largest was the $81-billion merger of Exxon and Mobil Oil). Compare that to WorldCom's takeover of MCI almost two years earlier for $37 billion. The transaction will be accounted for by the companies as a purchase and will be tax-free to shareholders. The companies propose to conclude the deal by December 31, 2000.

The Stock

Shareholders of Sprint (FON) will exchange each share of their stock for $76.00 worth of MCI/WorldCom stock, subject to a collar. The actual number of shares of MCI/WorldCom common stock to be exchanged for each Sprint (FON) share will be determined based on the average trading prices prior to the merger closing, but will not be less than 0.9400 shares (if MCI/WorldCom's average stock price exceeds $80.85) or more than 1.228 shares (if MCI/WorldCom's average stock price is less than $62.15). In addition, each share of Sprint PCS stock will be exchanged for one share of a new WorldCom PCS tracking stock (the terms of which will be equivalent to those of Sprint PCS) plus 0.1547 shares of MCI/WorldCom common stock.

On November 18, 1999, MCI/WorldCom declared a three-for-two stock split, to be effected as a 50% stock dividend on December 30, 1999. The exchange ratios under the original merger agreement had to be adjusted for this split. So, when the merger takes place, the number of MCI/WorldCom's shares to be exchanged for each Sprint (FON) share will be not less than 1.41 shares (if MCI/World-Com's average stock price exceeds $53.90) or more than 1.8342 shares (if MCI/WorldCom's average stock price is less than $41.43). The original deal also provided that each share of Sprint PCS would be exchanged for one share of a new WorldCom PCS tracking stock, but (as a result of the stock split) the premium with each new share was adjusted to 0.23205 shares of MCI/WorldCom common stock.

However, on December 14, 1999, Sprint announced a two-for-one split of Sprint PCS stock. The new shares will be issued on February 4, 2000, in the form of a dividend to shareholders of record on January 14, 2000. This split required a further adjustment to the original merger PCS premium ratio. Specifically, when the merger takes place, Sprint PCS stockholders will receive one share of WorldCom PCS stock plus 0.116025 shares of WorldCom stock for each Sprint PCS share that they own.

At the time of the announcement of the MCI/WorldCom stock split, MCI/WorldCom's stock was trading at $91 per share (Sprint FON was at $75.50), which was above the collar. If the merger would have occurred at that time, a Sprint (FON) shareholder would have received 94 shares of MCI/WorldCom stock (or, after the split, 141 shares of MCI/WorldCom stock) worth $8,554 (or $1,004 more than the trading value of the Sprint FON shares on that day). Sprint PCS shareholders would have received, in addition to the new WorldCom PCS shares, a premium per share worth $14.08 (Sprint

PCS traded that day at $91.50 per share). This deal, in other words, especially given the subsequent rise in the stock price, was very beneficial for Sprint FON and PCS shareholders. Indeed, $100 invested in Sprint's stock five years ago is now worth about $580 (compared to $200 for AT&T, and $300 for the S&P 500).

Regulatory Approvals

When it was first announced, though, the stock prices of both companies dipped. The commonly understood reason for the stock price decline was the expectation that the companies would encounter difficulty obtaining regulatory approval of the merger. This speculation was fueled by a rather terse statement released by William Kennard, the FCC Chairman, on October 5, 1999, which said: "American consumers are enjoying the lowest long distance rates in history and the lowest Internet rates in the world for one reason: competition. Competition has produced a price war in the long distance market. This merger appears to be a surrender. How can this be good for consumers? The parties will bear a heavy burden to show how consumers would be better off."

The hallmark of Bill Kennard's chairmanship at the FCC has been his concern for consumers, especially rural and minority consumers, as the national and world telecommunications market become more competitive and technology-driven. His oft-stated goal is to narrow what he calls the "digital divide" between consumers with access to the new technology and services, and those without such ready access. There have been a number of instances where, in my perception, MCI/WorldCom has not been a helpful partner in this effort. A prime example is MCI/WorldCom's dial-around long distance service (10-10-220), which is aggressively advertised as costing only 99 cents for up to 20 minutes.

The problem is that users who make calls of less than 20 minutes are charged the full 99 cents for each call, so a person who makes 10 one-minute calls (which often happens if, say, he or she reaches an answering machine) has to pay almost $10 for those 10 short calls. Irate consumers who've been caught in this trap have flooded the FCC with thousands of complaints, and I expect that Chairman Kennard will use the opportunity provided by the regulatory review of this merger to persuade MCI to change and improve its advertising. Kennard does not have authority to mandate such changes (unless the advertising is legally misleading), but he also doesn't have a time limit for approving (or rejecting) the merger. So he can simply delay any action until MCI/WorldCom "voluntarily" agrees to make the desired changes. It may not be fair, but it's the way the federal regulatory process works in such cases.

Sprint and MCI/WorldCom on November 17, 1999 formally filed their more than 300-page joint petition with the FCC for approval of the merger, arguing that it would speed the offering of new services (like wireless Internet access) without pushing up prices or reducing competition. The companies, by omission, seem to acknowledge that they may have to divest some Internet backbone facilities (which is what WorldCom had to do, at Sprint's urging, when it acquired MCI a year earlier), but rejected any further concessions. At the press conference announcing the filing, Sprint's General Counsel Rich Devlin was quoted (reminiscent of Dan Quayle) as saying "Beyond that, there's nothing thinkable in my mind."

A month after the joint application for approval of the merger was filed by Sprint and MCI/WorldCom with the FCC, the press obtained and revealed an internal FCC memorandum (that was dated October 21, 1999, a few weeks before the application was filed) that declared the merger to be an "intolerable" blow to competition. The author of the memo was reportedly Tom Krattenmaker, formerly an antitrust expert at the Justice Department, who was brought to the FCC (as a research director in the FCC's Office of Plans and Policy) a couple of years earlier to evaluate the mergers in the telecommunications industry (especially the Bell Company mergers). The memo reportedly raises two concerns: (1) the fact that the two companies both own substantial Internet "backbones" (i.e., high-speed data networks), and (2) the concentration in the marketplace that would result from the merger (about 80% of the nation's long distance business would be controlled by two companies — AT&T and the new WorldCom). Krattenmaker reportedly said in the memo that the market concentration "... will raise the most troublesome issue ...Any further consolidation among the major (long distance) providers would be intolerable, especially in its impact on residential subscribers."

The memo seemed to signal that the deal was in trouble, but I believe it should be discounted for a couple of important reasons. First, Krattenmaker himself reportedly began the memo with a disclaimer, saying, "I know very little about the 'proposed' merger ... and so am reluctant to say anything." Krattenmaker is a learned antitrust lawyer, and my dealings with him taught me that he's very thorough in his analysis and evaluation of the effect of business combinations. Thus it strikes me as peculiar that he would assert a conclusion in writing before having any of the facts. It's almost as though he was forced (over protests) to write this memo as support for a political scheme to position the FCC to extract concessions from the companies (and, it was subsequently revealed that Krattenmaker will leave the FCC in January 2000 to join a private law firm). Thus, the memo is likely to have little or no effect on the legal process of regulatory approval of the merger.

Second, the fact cannot be ignored that the FCC has never rejected a proposed merger in the telecommunications industry. And the merger of Sprint and MCI/WorldCom does not present sufficient public interest concerns to merit its rejection at this time. It's certainly true that the merger will increase concentration in the long distance marketplace, but that view looks backward (not forward) and ignores the dramatic changes taking place in the marketplace. Long distance as a distinct market (separate from local, wireless, data and even international service) is quickly disappearing. For instance, many wireless carriers (including Sprint PCS) have already adopted postalized rates; that is, they charge the same per call, regardless of whether it's local or long distance. Such changes in the way telephone service is provided and priced will certainly be rapidly and irreversibly accelerated as the Bell Companies are authorized to enter the long distance market in their regions (not to mention the similar impact as foreign carriers enter the U.S. domestic market).

Indeed, there's an argument that if the government doesn't allow Sprint and MCI/WorldCom to merge, it will place those companies at a disadvantage (insofar as, individually, they would not have the size, resources and breadth of services needed to succeed) in the marketplace of the not-too-distant future.

Thus, while the FCC will surely extract some concessions from the companies (like they did in the SBC-Ameritech merger), it's reasonable to believe that the merger will ultimately be approved.

However, the fact remains that the merger will substantially increase concentration in the long distance market; there would be left only two huge players (AT&T and WorldCom) controlling over 80% of the market. Robert Litan, former Justice Department antitrust lawyer (and now a director at the Brookings Institute), said "All other things being equal, that flunks every antitrust test you can think of." Joel Klein, the current Assistant Attorney General for Antitrust, has said only that the merger will get "a very serious and thorough review." The argument being made by the companies is that the market is changing rapidly; that long distance no longer is a distinguishable market, since competitors are or will soon (especially when the Bell Companies obtain long distance authority) offer "all distance" service (which, like Internet access, doesn't differentiate between local and long distance service). In any event, given the approvals of the monstrous mergers by the Bell Companies (each of which are outright monopolies in their markets), I think the government will have a very hard time not approving this deal.

Congress will also get involved before this deal is done. The Senate Judiciary Committee held a hearing on November 4, 1999, and called both Sprint CEO Esrey and MCI/WorldCom CEO Ebbers to testify. Esrey explained that the merger "will marshal the necessary talents and capabilities to meet the new larger scale challenges, and new, larger competitors." He also asserted that the new WorldCom will be able to achieve the objectives of the Telecom Act by breaking open the local monopolies and bring a distinctive competitor to the worldwide communications marketplace. Ebbers, in a subsequent editorial in the *Wall Street Journal*, more bluntly said, "There are two titans that have the potential to establish telephone hegemony — AT&T and the Bell operating companies. A merged MCI/WorldCom and Sprint represents the best hope for a strong and effective alternative …".

What Could Happen

That does not mean, though, that this deal will go through as originally conceived. Indeed, I believe a number of things can happen (and some very likely will). In the first place, I believe the FCC will extract a number of meaningful commitments from the companies (in addition to improving disclosures in MCI/WorldCom's advertising) as conditions for approval of the merger. A quick review of the conditions placed upon the SBC-Ameritech merger by the FCC — which includes things like agreeing to spend billions entering new markets, to serve previously unserved or under-served markets, etc. — provides great insight into what the FCC will want Sprint and MCI/WorldCom to "voluntarily" agree to implement. The question for MCI/WorldCom will become the cost of these commitments. Is it too much to proceed with the merger, or enough to cause the purchase price to be re-negotiated? Those, though, are typical questions in any merger requiring government approval.

What's not so typical is the possibility that competing offers for Sprint will emerge. BellSouth's initial offer was clearly not a lark. That company has to realize that it must link up with others in order to survive and thrive in the future, and that attractive partners are becoming scarce. There's a basis to argue that Sprint is BellSouth's last best chance to obtain the facilities, services, skills and market position needed to compete both domestically and internationally. So, even though BellSouth said that it wouldn't make a counter-offer, I think it should (and probably will) have second thoughts. Deutsche Telekom is in a similar position and, once it puts the humiliation of the Telecom Italia debacle behind it, will surely look long and hard at the need to acquire a U.S. carrier like Sprint. On the other hand, both companies (BellSouth & DT) certainly have the financial heft to await the completion of the Sprint merger and then make a run at the new WorldCom (and thereby acquire even greater capabilities). The next year or so will surely be interesting.

It will also be an anxious time for Sprint constituents. I think it's fair to assess the impact of the Sprint merger (whether it be with MCI/WorldCom, BellSouth, DT or any other possible suitor) on at least three different groups, each of which faces potentially and dramatically different consequences. The first group is Sprint's shareholders, and it's obvious that they will do very well (even more so if there's a subsequent bidding war for Sprint). That's clearly why the investment community welcomed the news of this merger so warmly. The other two groups don't fare so well, though.

Impact on Employees

Thousands of Sprint employees are placed in jeopardy by the MCI/WorldCom merger. If it goes through and MCI/WorldCom (as it has in past mergers) proceeds with internal consolidations, the harsh reality is that most of the administrative, network and marketing employees in Sprint's Long Distance Division will become redundant and likely be laid off. I need also to say that many Sprint employees are also stockholders (although many wish they had more stock than they do today), so this result is not necessarily bad news for them. Besides, most Sprint employees (at least in my experience) are very smart, skilled and energetic folks, who will surely go on to accomplish great things in the remainder of their careers, wherever that may be.

The attractiveness of Sprint's Local Division to MCI/WorldCom is the possibility of improved and low-cost access to local customers in some attractive markets (like Las Vegas, Tallahassee, Orlando, etc.), and MCI/WorldCom is surely planning to take advantage of those assets. But most of the Sprint Local Division properties — like Mansfield, Ohio, Hood River, Oregon, Bristol, Tennessee, etc. — are not attractive markets (regardless of the cost of access) and thus may be put on the auction block. Probably only Sprint PCS, which was obviously and initially the object of MCI/WorldCom's affections, will remain relatively intact post merger.

Thus, I suspect many Sprint employees are quietly yearning for a competing offer from another suitor. If Deutsche Telekom were to win Sprint, it would likely keep all of the current employees in the U.S. in place. From the standpoint of employees (and their families), that would surely be the best outcome. A takeover by BellSouth would also negatively impact fewer Sprint employees, since the only redundancies would the in the Local Division in the southeastern U.S. (where BellSouth already provides local telephone service).

Impact on the Community

The last group is the community of Kansas City, where Sprint is currently headquartered. Sprint is the largest single private employer, with about 17,000 employees, in the Kansas City area. It has occupied all or parts of about 60 office buildings at one time or another, and is presently constructing a 250-acre office complex in the Kansas City suburbs. Loss of the headquarters and those jobs will clearly have a negative impact on the Kansas City economy. I have no doubt that the community will recover (and that one or more companies like Sprint will grow and prosper in the years ahead), but the initial impact will be significant and unpleasant. Bernie Ebbers has said, and it's certainly true, that the new WorldCom will need more (but maybe different) employees in the future as the company grows, and it's possible that Kansas City could see (after an initial decline) an increase in the number of jobs there.

The Kansas City community is also taking some consolation in the announcement that Bill Esrey will, once the merger is consummated, become the Chairman of the Board of the new WorldCom, and his office will be in Kansas City. I don't mean to rain on the parade (or to mix metaphors), but this announcement should be taken with a grain of salt. After all, when WorldCom won the bidding war for MCI a couple years earlier, it was announced that MCI's CEO, Bert Roberts, would become Chairman of the new company; but he quickly disappeared from sight. It's entirely likely that the same fate awaits Bill Esrey (as well as Ron LeMay, who supposedly will become COO of the new company, also located in Kansas City). That will not be a hardship on Esrey; besides the fact that he'll reap $690 million worth of stock options when the merger is completed, he admits (in an article that appeared in the November, 1999 edition of *Ingram's* magazine) that, "I don't spend a lot of time in Kansas City … I spend a lot more time in Europe, a lot more time on the west coast and elsewhere, than I do here. Some of my friends on the coast have suggested I join their club, and I probably know more of the members there than I do at the golf club I'm a member of here. As a result, I am, regretfully, not that involved in Kansas City civically." I don't see the merger appreciably changing that situation.

Esrey admitted, in a December 9, 1999 keynote address to the Overland Park Chamber of Commerce annual meeting, that the $920-million office campus "won't be our corporate headquarters as it started out to be, but will be an enormously important part of the new company's operations." As a result, he said, "Kansas City will be the single biggest geographic unit of the new company going forward." He added that he was "very comfortable on the impact on our community in terms of opportunities, jobs, executives being good corporate citizens … I'm convinced that the Greater Kansas City and Overland Park area will be much better off as a result of it going forward." Typical of Esrey's attitude toward individuals (and his inclination to give non-specific assurances to quell controversy), he said, "The people who are concerned about job cuts going forward are really missing the point. Our problem is going to be how we get enough talented people to run a company that is growing that rapidly. We have 18,000 people in Kansas City today. That won't go down; it will probably go up, certainly over time. I think we all ought to relax and get on with the business at hand, and we'll all be just fine as a result of that."

Why did Sprint do it?

But, considering the negative impacts on employees (especially non-stockholding employees) and the community, it's reasonable to ask why did Sprint do it?

Bill Esrey has been quoted many times over the years as saying that he'd be interested in a merger with another company only if it could produce a return for shareholders that exceeded what he (and the Board of Directors) reasonably believed could be produced by the incumbent management team. The MCI/WorldCom offer (of, essentially, $76 a share) was a considerable premium over what Sprint (FON) stock was selling for (about $55 per share) at the time, but was it really that much more (if any) than what Sprint could have accomplished on its own over time? In fact, if you consider what's been achieved during the past 20 years and the long-term potential of the company (rather than simply calculating the short-term profits of shareholders), as well as the negative impacts on employees and the community, there's the basis for an argument that the MCI/WorldCom premium was not nearly enough.

Why, then, did Sprint agree to (indeed, solicit) the MCI/WorldCom merger at this time and for this price? I think a number of factors contributed to the decision. Global One was falling apart, and the extent and probable duration of the mounting losses were soon to be made public (Sprint's third quarter 1999 earnings, released on October 20, revealed Sprint's share of Global One's losses increased by 175% to 11 cents per share, from 4 cents per share for the same period a year ago). ION was horribly behind schedule (it was 16 months after the initial public announcement before the service was offered and then only in three selected cities), and the corresponding losses were piling up (Sprint's third quarter 1999 earnings showed losses attributable to ION increased by 250% to 7 cents per share, from 2 cents per share in the same period a year earlier). Once these developments became public and understood by the investment community, the price of Sprint's publicly traded stock was sure to suffer. Instead, the bad news was lost in the noise of the October 5 announcement of the MCI/WorldCom merger.

Also, if not more importantly, Sprint was in a strategically difficult position. More of the Bell Companies (in addition to Bell Atlantic in New York) will surely be allowed by state and federal (the FCC or Congress) governments to enter the competitive long distance market in the year 2000. Their entry, together with their massive size and market presence (especially since they continue to have virtual monopoly control over local access), will severely threaten the market shares and capabilities of competitive carriers like Sprint. And the key to success in the international marketplace has apparently not yet been found by anyone, but it's equally apparent that some carriers are bulking up in order to try to dominate that market; and Sprint, while having grown over the years to an impressive size, was still not nearly large enough to match the resources of those mega-carriers.

There are a number of industry commentators who assert that size is critical to survival in the global telecommunications market. I didn't subscribe to that notion. In fact, I thought that, given the vagaries of markets around the world, a single corporate approach was a handicap. Instead, I believed the carriers that succeed would be those that are good at taking advantage of multicultural alliances. However, natural market forces do not seem to always be controlling in the telecommunications industry today.

The BOCs, in an obvious effort to solidify their local monopoly positions, are merging and becoming much bigger. The combinations of SBC/PacTel/SNET/Ameritech and Bell Atlantic/NYNEX/GTE will each be, once completed, about $50 billion in annual revenues. That exceeds the Gross National Product of dozens of countries around the world. Their size virtually dictates that others must follow in-kind. The AT&T/TCI/MediaOne deal is an example of how competitors must both bulk up and try to develop alternatives to the BOC stranglehold over access to local customers. I personally think that AT&T is in for a rude awakening when they learn (as did STV in 1995) how much it will take to upgrade cable facilities to telephony standards.

Sprint was pursuing a strategy of trying to work with the BOCs to obtain much of the high-speed data access to local customers that will be needed to support ION, and to develop credible access alternatives as well. Sprint wanted cable companies to be required to provide open access to their coaxial (or fiber) to local customers, but couldn't count upon it. Instead, Sprint acquired some companies that have FCC licenses to provide local connections via fixed wireless. It's a technology (known as MMDS) that's not yet proven on a widespread basis, but it holds promise for comparatively inexpensive but high-speed digital access, especially in concentrated areas. Even though Sprint's strategy was promising, it was probably not enough to offset the need for size to compete against the other behemoths in the industry.

Some industry analysts predicted that Sprint's merger partner was likely to be a BOC (and BellSouth certainly made an initial credible effort), but there are (at least for the time being) some controlling legal obstacles. The fact is a BOC cannot acquire a long distance company (like Sprint) until it is authorized (under Section 271 of the Telecom Act) to provide in-region long distance service in all of its states, or it must divest the long distance assets in those states. I believe it could be several years before any BOC has accomplished such widespread approval, and it should be noted that the recent BOC mergers (which expand their local operations to more states) put each of them further behind that goal.

Some of the BOCs are trying to take advantage of the loophole in the Telecom Act that allows them to own less than 10% of a long distance carrier without having to satisfy the requirements of Section 271 (i.e., BellSouth's investment of 9.5% in Qwest, and US West's 9.5% deal with Global Crossing); but I don't see how such an arrangement could be attractive to Sprint. It either would encumber Sprint's ownership for a period of years (while the BOC sought to obtain in-region long distance authority) when the stock price could otherwise appreciate (especially if Sprint PCS and Global One reverse their losses during that time), or require the BOC to divest Sprint assets in its states (which is what Qwest will apparently do to acquire US West).

European carriers are beginning to understand the competitive market and realize that a significant presence in America is going to be essential for long-term success. Of the foreign carriers that potentially would be interested in acquiring Sprint, I believe DT is best positioned financially and strategically. DT is an impressive company. Not only does it have a tradition of operating and technological excellence, but it has the muscle and determination to get the job done. DT's upgrade of the entire telecommunications system in East Germany after the Berlin Wall came down is one of the most impressive feats in industrial history world-wide. They have proven they can do what they set out to do.

Domestically, the market — driven by technology — is also changing dramatically. The forecast that we'll soon move to "all distance" service (where customers will order and pay for bundles of local, wireless, long distance, international and data services) is likely a safe bet. Companies that cannot provide the entire package at attractive rates will surely be relegated to sub-markets. In that context, Sprint's initiative to merge its way into the role of a major player in the future, rather than simply accept a back seat, should be admired. But the question remains whether the pain that the MCI/WorldCom merger will inflict upon Sprint's employees is worth it?

My Opinion

I can't resist the urge to answer that question with my opinions. I have to admit that my wife and I own a fair number of Sprint FON and PCS shares, and that the impact of the merger with MCI/WorldCom on the price of that stock has enabled us to build our dream home in the country, to establish a private foundation to help some of our favorite charities and to enjoy the rest of our lives together in relative comfort. But, despite the positive impact upon our personal situation, I have to confess to serious reservations about the merger of Sprint and MCI/WorldCom. I've already covered the legal and strategic reasons for and against the merger. In addition thereto, I feel personal regret for the loss of a once great company.

Thousands of good and decent people worked very hard for decades to build Sprint into a dynamic, fast-growing, customer-focused, high-technology, aggressive yet compassionate company. Many of those same people who are still at Sprint have the capability and desire to continue to grow the company and reward stockholders (albeit, perhaps, not as fast as the merger will produce). Thus my preference would be to give them the time and opportunity to see what they can do. The merger, though, will never give them that chance. Instead, some of those talented employees will probably move on to other opportunities (some will surely start their own companies) and be successful, which represents yet another loss for Sprint.

My view is certainly clouded by my personal investment of blood, sweat and tears over three decades in the company, but I think the end of Sprint by merger with a former rival is in many respects no less than a shame. Even though WorldCom may, post-merger, preserve and use the Sprint brand in some markets, the essence and individuality of the company will (like US Telephone, Centel and others before it) soon be only a mere memory. Perhaps that's why I felt compelled to record the history of the company, as I know it, at this time.

CHAPTER NINE
Conclusion

GIVEN MY HISTORY with (and my obvious admiration for) the company, it's reasonable to wonder why I left. There were a number of reasons. The most immediate reason was a pending reorganization of the Law and External Affairs Department. I had been through a number of reorganizations, and always tried to make the best of them.

When Bill Esrey first asked me to become Senior VP of UTCI (and subsequently US Telecom) in 1984, I had responsibility for both the legal and governmental affairs functions. Del Knorowsky had the same responsibilities at GTE Sprint. So, when US Sprint was formed in 1986, he and I were asked to split the department, with me being responsible for just government affairs. I wasn't happy with the split, but tried to perform the function as best I could with rather limited resources (given the financial condition of the company at the time).

The functions were re-combined under the Executive VP-General Counsel when United Telecom took management control of Sprint in 1989. Rich Devlin and I were both considered for the job, and Rich got it (I distinctly remember that Ron LeMay notified me of that fact on October 10, 1989, by telephone while I was driving in from the airport). Again I was disappointed, but tried to support Rich and build a department that would position Sprint to have needed influence in government decisions affecting its business.

In late 1998, Rich decided to once again reorganize the department, this time moving people into new jobs seemingly for the sake of change. His stated purpose was to re-energize the department. But I was uncomfortable with change just for the sake of change, and I was particularly unhappy with the role that he had in mind for me. I'd like to believe, though, that my motivation wasn't purely personal. I was convinced that the proposed structure was not the most efficient or productive way for Sprint to conduct its government affairs.

I have to say also that my respect for my boss had substantially diminished. He and I had many stylistic and some substantive differences over that 10 years, but I was usually able to accept them (and continue to support him) because I believed that, at the core, he was a decent guy. However, near the end he started exhibiting the classic symptoms of mid-life crisis. Some asserted that his otherwise unexplained reorganization of the department was an attempt to compensate for the turmoil in his private life. I don't hold myself out as being a model for humanity, but family values are very important to me. I felt the best course of action was to simply remove myself from an unpleasant situation.

Moreover, I have to admit that I was tired. Almost 30 years of unceasing work had taken its toll. I learned early in my career that I was not the smartest person who worked for the company. I had been an average student in school and found that things did not always come easy on the job. So, with an ethic instilled by my father, I worked harder and longer than others just to keep up. Twelve-hour days and weekend work became routine. I got a reputation for being a workaholic, which (peculiarly) became a source of pride. I hardly ever took vacations and, consequently, short-changed my family.

Our family physician and friend, Dr. Tom Coppinger, repeatedly told me during annual exams that I needed to relieve stress, but I was sure that I knew better how to manage my life and career. As it turns out, he was absolutely right. Once I left the stress of work behind, I found that I felt (and slept) better. The time I spend with my family now is much more satisfying and rewarding than I could have imagined. I hope that others can learn from my mistake and be sure to always take time-off with their families. Don't wait until the end of your career. Instead, prolong your career by periodically re-charging your batteries.

Clearly the most important reason for leaving work was my family. My wife and I met when I was in Law School and she was in undergraduate school (the College of Agriculture) at the University of Missouri in Columbia, Missouri. We got married the summer after she graduated. During the first semester of my final year of Law School, we lived in a small duplex off campus and she worked in the Animal Husbandry Lab at the University. We soon learned, though, that two cannot live as cheaply as one, and we moved to Kansas City, where I went back to work full-time for United Telecom and finished Law School at night (taking an extra semester) at the University of Missouri-Kansas City. In the early years of our marriage, we both worked but had a lot of fun together. It was like an extended date. But I soon learned that marriage was a very special arrangement and obligation. Being married is probably the greatest challenge I've ever faced; it takes a daily (if not hourly) commitment to the feelings, well-being and success of each other. The lesson I learned was that the marriage was more important than me. The emotional and spiritual rewards of a good marriage are uniquely special and worth every ounce of effort.

My daughter's wedding a few years ago caused my wife and I to reminisce about our marriage a quarter of a century earlier and our life together. We did all the right things — we both worked, saved our money, bought a house, and so on — but never really understood why until our daughter was born. She became not only our pride and joy, but our reason for living. And life with her has been wonderful, but there hasn't been enough of it. So, after giving almost 30 years to Sprint, I wanted to give the next 30 years to my wife, my daughter and her husband. A job is important to financially support your family, but I've learned that family, and especially children, are the most important and rewarding aspects of life. I'm grateful that I'm now in a position to make up for all those years when my priorities were not in the proper order.

Almost immediately after I left the office for the final time, my former boss began to change and destroy most of what I had spent my career building. He changed the organization, reporting and working relationships, and virtually all other institutional memories that I had ever been a part of the company. What surprised me the most about this development, though, was my reaction. I wasn't upset, because (I think) I understood that's what normally happens in a management succession. In fact, the whole process struck me (one evening while I was walking our dogs and watching them urinate on top of the scent left by other dogs that previously passed that way), in a humorous way, as a form of "marking." But what provided me with the most comfort was the realization that the only lasting monument of any value to one's career is the friendships and personal relationships with really good people that develop over time. I was blessed to have hundreds of good friends at

Sprint, and an important part of my life is staying in touch with them and their families today.

In that regard, while I knew my departure from Sprint would be mourned by some, I also expected it would be celebrated by others (especially those who perceived me as a rival). But I was somewhat chagrined that the executive management chose to do nothing to recognize the 30 years that I gave to the company. No gold watch, no reception, nothing. I was pleasantly surprised (and moved) by the hundreds of e-mails, cards, letters and calls I received from current and former employees (some of which I did not realize I had affected during my tenure at Sprint), and from others both in and outside of the industry. But I was a little hurt by the fact that there wasn't a timely or even a kind word from some senior executives who I thought had been my friends. There seems to be very little of the Henson legacy of "family" left in some of the executive offices at Sprint these days.

Since the stock price is what enabled me to retire comfortably, though, I guess I'd prefer that executive management stay focused on running the company, rather than bemoaning the loss of just one employee. In that regard, while I've never been accused of being humble, I've honestly tried not to inflate my importance and contribution to the company. I've always liked the saying attributed to Vince Lombardi, to the effect that cemeteries are filled with people who were convinced that in life they were indispensable.

I don't mean by that to diminish the impact that some individuals can have, though. I used to believe that companies the size of Sprint were immune to the peculiarities of individuals. Paul Henson proved me wrong, because clearly the early organization reflected his personality and values. In later years, there was just as clearly a shift. We went from a company that was led by people who, in school, were captains of the football team to people who were captains of the debate team. The culture was more intellectual and deliberate, and less intuitive and spontaneous. That wasn't bad or wrong — indeed, I could argue that the company would never have achieved a higher level of success without it — but it was certainly different.

The many bosses I had over the years were just as different. Some, like Warren Baker, were great lawyers, but I also learned from some of my non-lawyer bosses. I had a few bosses who were more interested in padding their resumes and advancing their careers than understanding or accomplishing the work, and they moved on to other jobs relatively quickly. Art Krause, Sprint's current CFO, was probably the smartest boss I had. I had to work at a dead run, mentally, just to keep up with him. I obviously have great respect for Bill Esrey's vision and, although his views on human relations are different than mine, his mental toughness and record of success are admirable.

Ron LeMay is Bill Esrey's closest confidant and has parlayed his relationship and intelligence into the executive suite. But he's not regarded as an inspirational leader. There were times, when Sprint's stock was not doing well, that some investment analysts openly called for his departure. When Ron did leave for three months to become CEO of Waste Management in Chicago, there were mixed feelings. His publicly reported compensation package was irresistible, but why he opted for such a dramatic change in careers (after a lifetime in the telecommunications industry) defied logic and remains unexplained. Adding to the confusion were the circumstances of his return to Sprint (I was returning to Kansas City from addressing a meeting of the National Association of Attorneys General in Chicago the afternoon of October 29, 1998, when the company plane got a call to go back to Chicago to pick up Ron). But, in the end, Ron's relationship with Bill allowed him to return to Sprint as though nothing had happened.

At an officers' meeting conducted by Bill Esrey in early September, 1998 to promote "One Sprint" ideals (called the Catalyst Conference), members of executive management shared some personality assessments done by outside consultants. It was revealed that the executives all exhibited substantially the same personality traits — they all took a somber, rigorous, impersonal approach to business issues. They seemed proud and collegial. Many in the audience were uncomfortable, though, because that approach tended to minimize the importance of individuals, discourage creativity and prevent diversity.

The conformity among executives accounts in large measure, in my estimation, for the corporate culture of today's Sprint. While the company strives to achieve the legal minimums for employment diversity, it lacks a personal commitment to improve the lives of individuals and the betterment of mankind. I readily admit that Sprint is not (and should not be) an eleemosynary institution; but Paul Henson taught me about the importance of caring about people in the workplace, and I have always believed Sprint should have higher and more diverse people priorities.

The Big Picture

I'm inclined to conclude this tome by quoting from another speech. I'd like to think that I gained somewhat of a reputation during my Sprint career by giving entertaining if not interesting speeches. I must admit that, in the beginning, I (like most people) was petrified by public speaking. It was during one of Paul Henson's annual remarks to employees during a Christmas luncheon in the early 1970s that I decided to overcome those fears. Paul was such a mesmerizing speaker, and a genuine inspiration to me in many respects.

By my count, I made about 200 presentations to a variety of audiences — including regulators, legislators, industry groups, lawyers, foreigners, users, employees and investors — on regulatory issues, pending legislation, antitrust concerns, and the future of the business, during my 30 years at the company.

One of the speeches that I spent the most time thinking about and writing was the keynote presentation to the annual conference of the Nevada Telephone Association in Las Vegas in 1996. Others apparently liked it, because it was reproduced in the employee magazine, *Sprint Quarterly* (Vol. 6, No. 3). It was entitled "What in the World is Going On" and probably best summarizes the message I'm trying to convey here. In relevant part, I said:

"It's a hackneyed understatement to say that we're living in a world of change. The Telecommunications Act of 1996, effective this past February, brought some needed structure to the change in our business; but I contend that market forces, not legislation or regulation, are and will primarily define the future of our industry.

"In that regard, I believe the introduction of competition into local telephone markets was inevitable. The marketplace has for the past decade not only enjoyed but come to expect the benefits of long distance competition. Telecommunications consumers now demand choices among service providers, technology, quality and value.

"Congress went through great contortions to produce the first major change in telecommunications law in six decades, but (in my view) they simply conformed the law to marketplace reality.

"That's obviously my opinion; but one of the few benefits of being my advanced age and having my tenure in our industry is a perspective on historical developments, and most folks (like you) will tend to listen politely (regardless of whether I'm really full of hot air). So, I'm going to take advantage of your hospitality and regale you with what in the world I think is really going on.

"Let me start with the big picture; and I have to admit that my perspective has been influenced by listening to a number of historians and analysts who are a lot more perceptive and thoughtful than I. They've caused me to come to believe that the current condition of our country, our economy and especially our industry has been shaped by primarily two global events: the end of the Cold War and amazing technological advances.

"Following the end of World War II, the global economy — with only a few exceptions — was divided along the same lines as the Communist and Democratic governments. Communism in Russia and Eastern Europe recently failed because people living under repressive regimes demanded the freedoms available only in a Democracy. The result is that huge new markets, populated by hundreds of millions of consumers, have been opened to freedom, capitalism and global competition.

"This monumental change also produced a frustrating paradox. While almost half the world has now opted for economic Democracy (because they were envious of and wanted to enjoy the same things that Americans take for granted), there's been growing discontent among a meaningful numbers of workers in the United States due to the perceived lack of security in employment situations. We don't seem to want, in other words, what others in the world were willing to fight for. I believe the reason for this dilemma lies within the second global event that shaped our present situation.

"That event, as I mentioned earlier, is technology; specifically, communications technology. And I'm extremely proud to say that I believe Sprint played an important role in the introduction and deployment of that technology. In 1984, when Bill Esrey announced at our Annual Stockholders Meeting that United Telecom (Sprint's predecessor) was going to construct and operate a 23,000-mile, nationwide, all-digital fiber optic competitive long distance network, many in our industry scoffed. Indeed, AT&T laughed out loud and declared Sprint's plans a folly, since their copper wire network was entirely sufficient to carry all the long distance traffic that would ever be necessary in this country.

"I don't need to further embarrass AT&T with all the gory details (although I must admit that I enjoy doing so), so suffice it to observe that AT&T has subsequently converted much of its nationwide network to fiber optics. So has MCI, for that matter. But the point is that high-speed digital transmissions over optic networks has become the standard around the world today.

"The result is almost unfathomable amounts of information are transmitted around the world at the speed of light every minute of every day. We know more now faster than ever before. We used to find out about breaking news across the country or abroad by reading it in the newspaper the next morning. Today there are fewer newspapers and fewer readers, not because society is less literate, but (I believe) because much of the news is stale by the time it reaches print.

"All of this instant information means that consumers can and do react to innovations, promotions and other marketing initiatives of competitors around the world with greater ease and convenience than they used to hunt for a sale at the corner store. Successful competitors, therefore, have had to develop the culture and means to monitor and quickly react to relevant market developments.

"In that regard, one of the secrets of success seems to be the ability to sort through all of the available information and pay attention only to what's useful for your purpose. If you don't acquire that skill, you can easily get bogged down; there's just too much information that's readily available. Some statistician figured out that it's been since Biblical times that the smartest individual in the world could know all of the information then available. That is obviously impossible today. It's a little scary, but it's also exciting, challenging and in some measure responsible for our standard of living today.

"Admittedly, the world is not as comfortable a place to work as in years past. We used to have time to contemplate developments and react, but not any more. Companies with product cycles that require months or years are soon left in the dust by entrepreneurs that can do it in weeks or even hours. The landscape is sadly littered with the remains of once-grand companies that couldn't change or keep up with the competition. The resulting lack of employment security — especially the good ole days when you could count on some jobs for life — is terribly frustrating and hard on many people. But it's not going to get better. Indeed, it's likely to get even more intense.

"That's why companies need employees who come to work each morning and fight to maintain a competitive edge. People who are looking for job security, instead of a new and better way to satisfy customers, are an unaffordable luxury. A lot of people find the pressure caused by change unpleasant, but it's today's reality.

"Most Sprint employees, I believe, have learned to turn the anxiety caused by change into the energy to stay ahead of and beat the competition. There may be little security these days, but there's enormous personal and professional satisfaction in always trying to be *your best, staying focused on what's important and what you can do to improve it, and (as a result) winning.*

"I once heard Stephen Covey put it another way. Covey, as you likely know, is the author of the international best-selling book entitled "The 7 Habits of Highly Effective People." Hopefully you had the opportunity to see the PBS special on Covey's work, which Sprint was honored to sponsor last year. Covey has an almost ecumenical way of communicating some very powerful yet simple and personal messages.

"He says there are only three basic realities in the world; being (1) natural law (or, in my words, the inevitable), (2) change (which, in our industry, has become a daily factor), and (3) choice. Choice, according to Covey, is what distinguishes us as human beings. Faced with inevitability and change, we can choose how to act and react. We can choose values, relationships and ways of communicating that result in happiness, health and success ..."

I made my choices and have no real regrets. Sprint was a great experience, and I'll forever treasure the relationships I enjoyed with literally hundreds of good people throughout the industry. My career at Sprint also taught me a lot, and I'd like to think I made some contributions to the business, but probably my most meaningful accomplishment was providing employment, job satisfaction and a comfortable living to dozens (many of which I haven't mentioned by name) of decent, dedicated and caring people (and their families) over three decades. However, I've always felt that they gave me more than I gave them, and for that I will forever be grateful.

I have to admit, finally, to a longing for an end of the Sprint story that doesn't erase the magnificent history that I've tried to capture herein. The official Sprint biographers can and hopefully will write a more comprehensive history of the company. This book, as aforesaid, is only a personal collection of mostly fond memories of some exciting and fulfilling times. I hope it provides some insight and lessons for those who follow.

This was at a fund-raiser for Congressman Jim Talent (R-MO), who's running for Governor, at the Ritz-Carlton Hotel in Kansas City, on May 23, 1999. From left-to-right are New York Governor George Pataki, Rep. Talent, my wife (Linda), me, Kansas Governor Bill Graves, and Senator Kit Bond (R-MO).

Paul Henson (left) listens to Congressman Jim Slattery (D-KS) at a meeting with several officers in the United Telecom Boardroom to discuss telecom issues. Jim represented the 2nd Congressional District, ran for Governor in 1994 (against Bill Graves), and has been a good friend for a long time.

Linda and I with Senator Christopher S. (Kit) Bond (R-MO). We first met Kit in the early 1970's when he ran for State Auditor, and supported him in his races for Governor and U.S. Senator. He's a very special friend.

This was one of several annual conferences of the United Telecom Legal Department, when John Dodd (on the left in the back row) was General Counsel. Some of the folks in the group are Don Jensen, Corporate Secretary (far left), Dub Hill (4th from the right, first row), Dick Croker (back row, in the middle) and me (2nd from the right, second row).

This was a Revenues Conference (of the folks that worked on rate cases) in Kansas City (when I was in Tennessee, circa 1978). Some of the folks in the group are Art Krause (back row, in the middle), Dick Cashwell (back row, far right), Bill Roche (2nd row, 3rd from left), Dub Hill (1st row, middle), Dick Croker (1st row, far right) and me (1st row, far left).

At the top is the in-house celebration on the day (July 1, 1986) that we launched US Sprint. In the middle (left to right) are Bill Esrey, Woody Overton (who headed Senator Tom Eagleton's KC office, then came to us and now heads the GSA Office in KC), and me. At the bottom is Bob Snedaker preparing to testify before a Congressional Committee; that's me to his left (that was back when you could smoke in government buildings).

These were taken at a fundraiser for Jim Slattery in our home. At the top, with Jim, is Ellen D'Amato, Sprint's VP-State Regulatory, a special friend. At the bottom, Jim is with my secretary, Sharon Rhodes (she married Gerry, a Sprint VP-Marketing, who then became an executive with Aerial Communications and moved her — much to my consternation — to Chicago).

These are from a political rally at Sprint, when candidates in several state and federal elections addressed employees. At the top left, I'm with Jill Docking, who ran against Sam Brownback for Senator from Kansas. At the top right is Bekki Cook, Secretary of State of Missouri. At the bottom, I'm with Bill Washington, Sprint's Public Affairs Officer and a good friend for many years.

At the top is the group that gave Congressman Vince Snowbarger (R-KS) a tour of the site of the new Sprint campus. From the right is me, Bill Roche, Vince and Faye Manker, Sprint's VP in charge of construction. On the far left is Mike Murray, Sprint's Government Affairs Director in Kansas (and former staffer for Congresswoman Jan Meyers, Vince's predecessor). The photo at the bottom was taken at a reception that Sprint hosted for Karen McCarthy (D-MO) when she was first elected to Congress. Left to right is me, Karen and former Kansas City Mayor Dick Berkley (it's unusual to get a picture of Dick; he's usually on the other side of the camera).

This was also at a political rally for Sprint employees. At the top, I'm with Dennis Moore, who defeated Vince Snowbarger to represent the 3rd District of Kansas in the 106th Congress. At the bottom is Kathleen Sebelius, the Insurance Commissioner of the State of Kansas. She's from a well-known political family, is a delightful young lady and is regarded as a rising star in state politics.

At the top is me with Senator Pat Roberts (R-KS) visiting the Sprint campus construction site. Pat represented the 1st Congressional District of Kansas for many years, and replaced Senator Nancy Kassebaum when she retired. He's a graduate of Kansas State University, and is giving me a hard time about my tie (because of the MU colors). At the bottom, I'm with Mark Bredemeier, who was a candidate for Missouri Attorney, at a Sprint rally. Mark's a bright young lawyer, who's been a good friend for several years.

At the top, Linda and I are visiting with Howard Baker. It was a fundraiser for Senator Danforth in Kansas City, and at the time Baker was Chief of the White House staff for President Reagan. He subsequently headed the Long Distance Coalition during the debates over the Telecommunications Act, and married former Kansas Senator Nancy Kassebaum. I've admired him for a long time. At bottom, Linda and I are with Pete Wilson at a May 1988 fundraiser in Kansas City, when he ran for the Senate (and pledged not to resign and run for Governor of California).

The top two photos are of the news conference when Sprint announced that it was going to move to a new building near Kansas City's Country Club Plaza. The developers subsequently declared bankruptcy and the deal fell apart. Sprint ended-up in parts of almost 60 office buildings around Kansas City, which was one of the reasons for building the new campus. In the top photo, Congressman Alan Wheat (D-MO) is at the microphone. Seated at the head table second from the right is Charles Skibo; to his right is Bill Esrey. Dick Berkley, Mayor of Kansas City, is in the middle photo. In the bottom photo, Senator Danforth (R-MO) greets Sprint employees. I'm on the left, and Woody Overton is on the right.

Two dinners twenty years apart. At the top is a table at the banquet of the 1978 annual Virginia Independent Telephone Association (VITA) convention at The Homestead. On the left are Louis & Madelon Corning (Louis was VP-Revenues at the UTS-Southeast Group); in the middle is me (with a little more hair) and Linda; and on the right are Ned and Bunny Addison (Ned headed the Virginia Corporation Commission staff). At the bottom, Gary Forsee (on the right) and his lovely wife Sherry (on the left) came to Paris, France (from Global One's office in Brussels) to have dinner with us in December, 1998. The River Seine is in the background. Both were wonderful evenings with very special friends.

A White House photographer recorded the 1994 meeting between (from left to right) Vice President Gore, Bill Esrey, Jim Lewin and me, when we discussed the Global One venture with FT & DT, as well as pending federal telecommunications legislation.

This is the team of folks that worked on the regulatory approvals for the partnership with FT & DT. On the bottom row (from left to right) are Ted Krause (head of FT's Washington Office), Leon Kestenbaum (Sprint's VP-Federal Regulatory in D.C.), Dr. Klaus Mai (head of DT's Washington Office), Grover Bynum (Sprint's federal legislative director) and me. In the top row are Kevin Sullivan (attorney with King & Spadling, representing Sprint), Dick Juhnke (Sprint's federal regulatory director), Werner Hein and his law partner (representing DT), Sydney Shaw (Sprint's P.R. director), FT's outside counsel, Jim Lewin and Sally Smith (Sprint's VP and AVP for Federal legislative matters in D.C.). The photo was taken in Sprint's D.C. Office on the day the FCC approved the deal in December 1995.

This was a fundraiser for Congressman Vince Snowbarger in Kansas City. From left to right are Senator Sam Brownback (R-KS), Charlton Heston, my wife (Linda), and Vince. I was out-of-town and couldn't attend, but that didn't stop Linda (who wouldn't miss the opportunity to meet her favorite "hunk").

This may be my favorite photo. I was introducing Senator Danforth (R-MO) to a gathering of US Sprint employees (circa 1987). I have been a big fan of his since I first met him when I was in Law School at the University of Missouri (when he was running to become the first Republican in the state to be elected Attorney General since Reconstruction). He has a magnificent record of public service, and I tried to capture it in my introduction; but he responded with his usual modesty and humor. We shared a good laugh.

This was at a fundraiser for Senator Ashcroft (R-MO) in Kansas City. From left to right are Senator Jeffords (R-VT), Senate Majority Leader Lott (R-MS), me, Ashcroft and Senator Craig (R-ID). Shortly afterwards, the four Senators — know as the "Singing Senators" — performed in Branson, Missouri (they're entertaining, but they shouldn't quit their day jobs …).

This photo was taken during a break at the April, 1995 Sprint federal legislative conference at Vail, Colorado. Lying in the snow are House Telecom Subcommittee Chairman Jack Fields (R-TX) and Bill Esrey. On the left of the back row are Mike Regan and Kathey Reid (House Telecom Subcommittee staffers, and great friends) and Julie Esrey. I'm in the middle of the back row (with sunglasses) between Bill Barloon and Grover Bynum.

This was another fundraiser in Kansas City for Congressman Vince Snowbarger (R-KS). From left to right are Speaker of the U.S. House Newt Gingrich (R-GA), Linda, me and Vince. Gingrich was certainly controversial, and history probably will find him to be a better revolutionary than a leader; but I found him to be very bright, articulate, committed and a little shy.

This photo was taken at a dinner for President Clinton in Washington, D.C. From left to right are Jim and Carol Lewin, me, Ann Bingaman, Assistant U.S. Attorney General —Antitrust (and wife of the Senator from New Mexico), and Phil Verveer, Washington, D.C. attorney with Willke, Farr & Gallagher (and a good friend).

159

This photo appeared on the front page of the February 24, 1986 issue of Communications Week. *The setting was a hearing before the U.S. House Telecom Subcommittee, then chaired by Rep. Wirth (D-CO). The witnesses on this panel were (left to right) Bill McGowan (Chairman of MCI), Al Partol (Executive VP-Regulatory for AT&T) and me. The caption under the photo identified us, in order, as "Wary, Wealthy, Weary."*

From left to right, Senator Kit Bond (R-MO), me and Senate Majority Leader Bob Dole (R-KS), at a fundraiser for Kit in Kansas City.

While flying from his beloved California to Washington, D.C., President Reagan had Air Force One land at the Kansas City Municipal Airport to attend a fundraiser to help Kit Bond's campaign for the U.S. Senate. Linda didn't believe me when I called to tell her that she was going to meet the President; then she got mad at me because she only wore a cotton dress (such things, according to Linda, are usually my fault).

From left to right, Senator Kit Bond (R-MO), me, Secretary of Defense (under President Bush, during Desert Storm) Dick Cheney, and Senator Ashcroft (R-MO). Cheney's an impressive guy; I wish he'd run for President.

163

Backstage before the Rolling Stones concert on October 23, 1997, in the Jack Kent Cooke Stadium in Washington, D.C. I'm on the far left (not dressed nearly warm enough). It was a gas, gas, gas …

Horsing around. At the top, my daughter (Heather) is riding her first horse (McCoy's Pride) during the PRCA Rodeo at Benjamin Stables in Kansas City in 1987. She's leading the winner of an event in a victory lap around the rodeo ring, carrying the sponsor's flag. The bottom family photo was taken the day before my daughter was married (to Sam Lind) in 1997. The horse (Kartel) is a beautifully trained (by Serendipity Farms) purebred Arabian, with a sparkling personality, who has become a real member of the family. Heather is holding our dog Dinka, and Linda is holding Louie (my wife and daughter named the dogs, not me). Linda and I have bought some acreage south of Kansas City, are building our retirement ranch, and plan to raise horses and dogs.

Former President George Bush came to Kansas City to support the re-election of Senator John Ashcroft (with his wife, Janet). Both Bush and Ashcroft are men of great integrity and high moral principles. Linda and I both wish more politicians were like them.

John R. Hoffman

ABOUT THE AUTHOR

John R. Hoffman was born in 1945 in Rochester, New York. He grew up in Rochester and Chicago, and his family moved to Kansas City when he was in high school. He earned a B.A. Degree in History and Political Science in 1967 at Washburn University in Topeka, Kansas (and spent a semester at the University of Copenhagen in Denmark), and a J.D. Degree at the University of Missouri School of Law, Kansas City, Missouri. He's admitted to practice law before the Supreme Courts of Missouri (1971), United States (1975), Tennessee (1976) and Kansas (1980). He began his career at Sprint as a law clerk in 1967 (when the company was called United Utilities, Incorporated), and held various legal and management positions in successor and subsidiary companies. He served as Senior Vice President-External Affairs of Sprint Corp. from 1989 until he retired in 1999. He serves or has served on a number of corporate, civic and charitable boards, including the FCC's North American Numbering Council & Network Reliability Council, Kansas City Friends of the Zoo, Bishop Miege High School Foundation, United Telephone Company of the Northwest, Compaq Computer's Telecommunications Advisory Board, Kansas City Economic Development Council, Trinity Lutheran Hospital, Competitive Telecommunications Association, Kansas City Chapter of Young Audiences, Kansas City/CORO Foundation, and Consolidated Fire District No. 2 of Johnson County, Kansas. He's married to the former Linda Lee Moore, and they reside in Mission Hills, Kansas. Their daughter and son-in-law, Heather Anne and Samuel N. Lind, reside in Leawood, Kansas.

INDEX

A

Addison, Ned & Bunny 151
Aerial Communications 144
AirTouch 70
Alarcon, Javier Lozano 105
Alden, Ray 22
Alestra 105
AllTel 15
American Telephone Company 2
AmeriSource 13
Ameritech 50, 71, 102-103, 119-120, 125
AOL-Time Warner 1
Ashcroft, Senator John .. 75-76, 156, 163, 166
AT&T   14, 16-18, 20-21, 25-26, 29, 41, 43, 45,
    55, 62, 64, 67, 69-70, 84-85, 88, 98, 103,
    105, 118, 120, 125, 135
AT&T 90
Avantel 105

B

Baker, Howard 53, 57-58, 149
Baker, Warren 7, 9, 132
Baird, Zoe 49
Barloon, Bill 157
Barshevsky, Charlene 104
Bell, Alexander Graham 2, 63, 92
Bell Atlantic 70-71, 102, 124-125
Bell Operating Companies (BOCs) 22,
    25, 64-66, 102, 119-120, 124
BellSouth 89, 102, 113-114, 121-122, 126
Bergen, Candice 44-45
Berkley, Dick 109, 146, 150
Berlin Wall 126
Bingaman, Ann 159
Bischoff, Carol Ann 77
Bishop Miege High School 169
Bliley, Rep. Tom 76-77
Bond, Senator Kit .. 75-76, 140, 161, 162, 163
Bon, Michel 88, 114
Booz, Allen & Hamilton 26
Boucher, Rep. Rick 58
Bowman, Pasco 98
Bozell Sawyer Miller Group 67
Brady, Nicholas 16
Braniff Airlines 17
Brauer, Kevin 93
Bredemeier, Mark 148
British Telecom 84
Brooks, Rep. Jack 41, 75
Brophy, Ted 27, 39
Brown, Cleyson L. 2

Brownback, Senator Sam 145, 154
Brown, Dick 50
Brown, Murphy 44-45
Brown Telephone Company 2
Browning, Charles 11
BT 70
Buck the Horse 20
Burch, Dean 77
Bush, George 44, 166
BusinessWeek Magazine 20, 94
Bynum, Grover 49, 153, 157

C

Cable & Wireless 46, 50
Cashwell, Dick 11, 142
Catalyst Conference 133
Cauley, Leslie 41
Central Telephone Company (Centel) 14, 47-49,
    127
Cheny, Dick 163
Cisco Systems 94
Cleaver, Rev. Emanuel 78
Clement, Bobby 9
Clinton, Bill 49, 78-79, 97, 108, 159
Clinton, Hillary 72
Cofetel 105
Coleman, Rep. Tom 75
Comcast 82
Commerce Department 85
Compaq Computer Corp. 53, 169
CompTel 35, 169
Consolidated Fire District No. 2 169
Consumer Federation of America 71
Consumers Union 71
Continental Telephone Company 4
Control Data Corp. 15
Conyers, Rep. John 43
Cook, Bekki 145
Cooper, Mark 71
Corning, Louis & Madelon 11, 151
CORO Foundation 169
Coppinger, Dr. Tom 130
Covey, Stephen 137
Cox Cable 82
CPNI 106-107
Craft, Jack 75
Craig, Senator 156
Cray Computers 15
Croker, Dick 141, 142
CSX Railroad 19

D

Dallas Cowboys 51
D'Amato, Ellen 74, 144
Danforth, Senator Jack 39, 43, 75, 78, 150, 155
DARPA 91
Daschle, Tom & Linda 53
Dennis, Patricia Diaz 74
Deutsche Telekom ... 84,87-90, 104, 113-114, 121-122, 126
Devlin, Rich 118, 129
Digital Equipment Corp. 53
Dillon Read & Co. 16, 83
Dingell, Rep. John 73
Docking, Jill 145
Dodd, John 141
Dole, Senator Bob 78-79, 161
DSL 94
DWDM 93

E

Eagleton, Tom 143
Ebbers, Bernie 113, 115, 120, 122
EDS 41, 49, 83
E-Rate 99
Esrey, Bill 1, 16-18, 20, 31, 35, 37, 39, 42, 47, 51, 56, 60, 78-79, 82-85, 87, 89, 113-114, 120, 123-124, 128, 133, 135,143,150,152, 157
Esrey, Julie 60, 157
Esrey, Todd 16
Essential Elements 61
Exxon 115

F

FBI 86
Federal Communications Commission 14, 15, 18, 25, 27, 68, 81, 84-85, 97-98, 100-102, 104, 107, 110, 115, 117-121
Federal Computer Week 43
Ferris, Charles 77
Fields, Rep. Jack 60-61, 77, 157
Foote, Cone & Belding 29
Forbes, Kip 33
Forbes, Steve 33, 78
Forsee, Gary 32, 87-89, 151
Forsee, Sherry 151
Fowler, Mark 77
France Telecom 84, 87-89, 104, 114
Frazee, Jack 49
Friends of the Zoo 169
Frisby, Russell 35
Frontier Corp. 70, 110
FTS 2000 .... 40, 74

FTS 2001 43
Fuciu, George 27
Furchtgott-Roth, Harold 77

G

GATT 104
Greenbriar Resort 19
General Services Administration 40
Greene, Judge Harold 21, 63
Gingrich, Rep. Newt 76, 158
Gioia, John 43
Global Crossing 70, 126
Global One 85, 87, 114, 124, 126
GM 83-89
Goldman, Don 48
Goldwater, Senator Barry 76
Gore, Al 43, 71, 79, 99, 152
Graves, Governor Bill 78, 139
Greene, Judge 103
GTE 4, 21, 25, 27, 39, 62, 70-71, 125
GTE Sprint 26-27, 29, 31, 35, 62, 74, 129

H

Hallmark Cards 3
Hann, David 30
Hasselwander, Alan 110
Hawthorne, Denee 53
Heeter, Jim 109
Hein, Werner 153
Helo, Carlos Slim 105
Henson, Betty 4
Henson, Paul 1,3-5, 16-17,27,39,132, 134, 139
Henson, Susan and Beth 3
Heston, Charlton 154
Hill, W.W. "Dub" 9, 141, 142
Hoffman, Heather 165, 169
Hoffman, John 169
Hoffman, Linda 138, 140, 149, 151, 154, 158, 162, 165, 166, 169
Hoffman, Raymond E. 5
Hoffman, Raymond O. 5
Hollings, Peatsy 78
Hollings, Senator Ernest 73, 78
Horton, Rep. Frank 43
H&R Block 50
Hubbell, Webster 85-86
Hundt, Reed 77, 104
Hunt, Lamar 7

I

Iacocca, Lee 20
IBM 22

Independent Counsel 86-87
Ingram's Magazine 123
International Communications Association 73
ION 90-94, 124-125
Irving, Larry 77
ISACOMM 17
ISDN 94

J

Jagger, Mick 52
JCS2000 93
J.D. Power Award 63
Jeffords, Senator 156
Jenkins, Sharon 18
Jensen, Don 141
Johnson, Rocky 32, 39
Joint Board 99
Juhnke, Dick 153
Justice Department 21, 27, 48, 71, 72, 85-86, 101-102, 115, 116, 120
J. Walter Thompson 29, 44-45

K

Kansas City Chiefs 7
Kansas City Economic Development Council 169
Kansas City Star 6
Kartel 165
Kassebaum, Senator Nancy .. 44, 57, 148, 149
Keating, Deb 34
Keithley, Jay 74
Kelly, Tim 50, 52
Kemp, Jack 78
Kennard, Bill 77, 117-118
Kerrey, Senator Bob 76-77
Kestenbaum, Leon 74, 153
Kimmelman, Gene 71, 73
King & Spaulding 85
Kinnard, Wood 19
KKR & Co. 95
Klein, Joel 120
Knorowsky, Del 129
Krattenmaker, Tom 118-119
Krause, Art 17, 27, 133, 142
Krause, Ted 153
Kreamer, J.G. "Skinny" 3
Kurtze, Al 49

L

LCI 70
Leland, Rep. Mickey 77
LeMay, Ron 32, 83, 89, 103, 123, 129, 133

Levin, Blair 77
Lewin, Jim 41, 43, 56, 75, 79, 85-86, 152, 153, 159
Lightnet 19
Lind, Sam 165, 169
Line Costs Task Force 34
Litan, Robert 119
Local Number Portability 110-112
Lombardi, Vince 132
Lott, Senator Trent 156
Lucas, John 19
Lucier, Phil 4

M

Mai, Klaus 153
Manker, Faye 146
Manning, Danny 39
Manuel, Patti 32
Markey, Rep. Ed 77
McCain, Senator John 76, 109
McCarthy, Rep. Karen 76, 146
McDonald, Bill 19, 20
McGowan, Bill 30, 160
MCI 1, 25, 27, 29, 42-43, 49, 55, 67-69, 84, 105, 116, 135
MCI/WorldCom 1, 37, 70, 89, 95, 113-124, 127
McKinsey & Co. 16, 17
MediaOne 70, 125
Meyers, Rep. Jan 76, 146
MMDS 94, 125
Mobil Oil 115
Moir, Brian 73
Moore, Rep. Dennis 147
Murray, Mike 76, 146
Musgrave, Bill 33

N

NARUC 34
National Association of Attorneys General 133
National Football League 50-51
National Journal 71
NCAA Final Four Tournament 39
Neel, Roy 79
Nespola, Rich 34
Ness, Susan 72
Network Reliability Council 169
Nevada Telephone Association 134
NextWave 82
North American Numbering Council 110, 112, 169
North American Numbering Plan 111
NTIA 77, 85

NYNEX 70-71, 125

O

Odum, Shea 18
Olivetti 88
Overland Park Chamber of Commerce 123
Overton, Woody 143, 150
Oxley, Rep. Mike 60

P

PacTel 70-71, 125
Palmisano, Roseanne 33
Paranet 50
Pardo, Jamie Chico 105
Partol, Al 160
Pataki, Gov. George 138
Patrick, Dennis 77
Pfeiffer, Eckhard 53
PICCs 100-101
Powell, General Colin 77
Powell, Michael 77
Pressler, Senator Larry 56
Prigmore, Don 31
PTAT 45

Q

Quayle, Dan 44, 78, 118
Quality Program 35
Qwest 70, 103, 126

R

RadioShack 51-52
Rand McNally 81
Reagan, President Ronald 16, 57, 149, 162
Regan, Mike 77, 157
Reid, Kathy 157
Republican National Convention 43-44
Richey, Linda 78
Rhodes, Sharon & Gerry 144
RJR 95
Roberts, Bert 123
Robertson, Cliff 44
Roberts, Senator Pat 148
Roche, Bill 142, 146
Rogers, Will 57
Rolling Stones 52, 164
Rucker, Kevin 19

S

SAGA 72
SBC 70-71, 74, 102-103, 119-120, 125
Schell, Ted 48

Scott, Dave 48
Scupin, Carl A. "Skip" 1, 2
Sebelius, Kathleen 147
Shaw, Sydney 153
SHL Systemhouse 49
Sikes, Al 75, 77
Simon, Greg 71
Skibo, Charles 28, 31, 33, 150
Slattery, Jim 139, 144
SLCs 100-101
Smail, Ed 8
Smith, Sara H. (Sally) 75, 78, 153
Snedaker, Bob 27, 31, 143
Snowbarger, Rep. Vince 76, 146, 154, 158
Sommer, Ron 88, 114
South Carolina PSC 10
Southern New England Telephone 19, 70, 125
Southern Pacific Railroad 25
SP Communications 25, 27
Sprint Canada 90
Sprint PCS 49, 51, 83-84, 116-117, 119, 122, 126
Sprint Quarterly 134
Sprint Spectrum 83
STET 84
Stewart, Alan & Cappy 18
Strategic Review Challenge Team 48
Strickling, Larry 110
Stromberg Carlson 4, 5
Strowger, Almon B. 3
STV 49, 82-83, 87-88, 125
Sukawaty, Andy 83
Sullivan, Kevin 153
Sunshine, Steve 85
Synar, Rep. Mike 57-58

T

Talent, Rep. Jim 138
Tandem Computers 53
Tandy Corp. 51
Tauzin, Rep. Billy 73, 76
TCG 70
TCI 70, 82, 125
Telecom Italia 88
Telecommunications Act of 1996 .... 55, 58-73, 97-101, 103, 107-108, 134
Telematics 35
Telenet 14, 31, 84
Telex 51
Tellabs 94
Telmex 89, 105-106
TELRIC 100

174

Tennessee PSC 9
Thomas, Justice Clarence 75
360 Degrees Communications 15
Treasury Department 85
Trinity Lutheran Hospital 169

U
Uninet 14
Unisource 90
United Computing Systems 15
United Inter-Mountain Telephone Company 8, 58
United Telecommunications, Inc. 13, 14, 15-16, 22, 62, 74, 129, 131, 135
United Telecom Communications, Inc. 17, 129
United Telephone Company of the Northwest 169
United Telephone & Electric 2
United Telephone System 3, 11, 16
United Telesentinel 13
United TeleSpectrum 14
United Utilities, Incorporated 2, 6, 169
University of Copenhagen, Denmark 169
University of Missouri-Columbia 130
University of Missouri-Kansas City . 131, 169
Uniwatch 13
Upper East Tennessee 10
Upson, Don 43
US Sprint 14, 25, 29-30, 34, 36, 39, 62, 74, 83, 129
USTA 62
US Telecom 17, 19, 22, 24, 27, 29, 31, 35, 39, 129
US Telephone 17, 18, 27, 62, 74, 127
U.S. Trade Representative 103, 104
US West 70, 103, 126

Utelcom 13
UTS-Southeast Group 7, 10
UUNet 114

V
VanDeerlin, Rep. Lionel 55
Verveer, Phil 72, 159
Vodafone 70

W
Wall Street Journal 41
Walston, Wayne 74
Ward, Sela 45
Washburn University 169
Washington, Bill 145
Waste Management 89, 133
Watson, Ben 48
Western Electric 4
Wheat, Rep. Alan 150
Wheeler, Chuck 43
White House 86
Wholstetter, Charles 4
Wiley, Dick 77
Williams, Mont 34
Willke, Farr & Gallagher 72
Wilner, Carl 85
Wilson, John 9
Wilson, Pete 149
Wirth, Rep. Tim 160
Wolf, Luther 11
WorldCom 84, 115, 118, 120, 123, 127
Wright, Sheryl 28
WTO Basic Telecom Treaty 66, 103-104

X, Y, Z
Young Audiences 169